# Beyond
# Differentiated
# Instruction

# Beyond Differentiated Instruction

## Jodi O'Meara

**CORWIN**
A SAGE Company

*For information:*

Corwin
A SAGE Company
2455 Teller Road
Thousand Oaks, California 91320
(800) 233-9936
Fax: (800) 417-2466
www.corwin.com

SAGE Ltd.
1 Oliver's Yard
55 City Road
London EC1Y 1SP
United Kingdom

SAGE India Pvt. Ltd.
B 1/I 1 Mohan Cooperative
 Industrial Area
Mathura Road, New Delhi 110 044
India

SAGE Asia-Pacific Pte. Ltd.
33 Pekin Street #02-01
Far East Square
Singapore 048763

Printed in the United States of America.

*Library of Congress Cataloging-in-Publication Data*

O'Meara, Jodi.
Beyond differentiated instruction/Jodi O'Meara.
    p. cm.
Includes bibliographical references and index.
ISBN 978-1-4129-8203-0 (pbk.: alk. paper)
   1. Individualized instruction. 2. Cognitive styles in children. 3. Mixed ability grouping in education. 4. Elementary school teaching. I. Title.

LB1031.O49 2010
371.39'4—dc22                                    2009047379

This book is printed on acid-free paper.

10   11   12   13   14   10  9  8  7  6  5  4  3  2  1

| | |
|---|---|
| *Acquisitions Editor:* | Hudson Perigo |
| *Associate Editor:* | Julie McNall |
| *Editorial Assistant:* | Allison Scott |
| *Production Editor:* | Cassandra Margaret Seibel |
| *Copy Editor:* | Adam Dunham |
| *Typesetter:* | C&M Digitals (P) Ltd. |
| *Proofreader:* | Susan Schon |
| *Indexer:* | Gloria Tierney |
| *Cover Designer:* | Michael Dubowe |

# Contents

# *Acknowledgments*

This book would not have been possible without the belief and encouragement from my editor, Hudson Perigo. Thank you so much for recognizing my potential and providing gentle encouragement along the way. Your enthusiasm and excitement fueled my fires and determination. Thank you for giving me this opportunity to grow and experience so much excitement and success.

I would like to thank so many people in the field of education who have helped me gain the knowledge, experience, and confidence to write this book.

Thank you to Donnajo Smith from the Florida Department of Education for seeing the spark in me long ago and recognizing my passion for learning and for the education of students identified as gifted. Also, thank you for inviting me into so many conversations and experiences to expand my thinking and gain much of the knowledge needed to complete this book.

Thank you to Dr. Christine Weber from the University of North Florida for your unwavering belief in me and providing me opportunities and challenges to expand my learning and collaboration efforts.

Thank you to Dr. Mary Little of Response to Intervention Teaching Learning Connections. You have such passion and vision. I have been so fortunate to be a part of your team and your visions. Thank you for the opportunities you have provided me for the past eight years. You have been there to watch me grow!

Thank you to Dr. Shelby Roberson, associate director of Mathematics for Response to Intervention Teaching Learning Connections and, more important, my friend. You have provided me with so many learning and teaching experiences as well as ideas, allowing me to organize my thinking for this book. Your support and friendship have helped me remain patient, optimistic, and smiling.

Thank you to Ron Russell, director of Exceptional Student Education, Manatee County, FL. As a friend and supervisor, you have given me the nourishment, space, and confidence to grow and share what I know.

Thank you to Maryann Ahearn, director of the Florida Diagnostic and Learning Resources System (FDLRS), for your leadership and vision. You have been a wonderful role model for me as an educational leader.

Thank you to the thousands of teachers and students whom I have both taught and learned from. The students make the teacher and the collaboration among teachers makes the special profession of education an art as well as a science.

On a personal note, I need and want to thank Russell Schall, who has always believed that I could do anything and has been my biggest supporter since the idea first started. You have been there through the entire process of hard work and sweet success. I would have given up if it weren't for you.

Thank you also to my grandparents, Fred and Ruth Choate, who have been my biggest fans. You have been the living voice of my dad. I am so pleased to make you proud.

Finally, thank you is nowhere near enough to begin to speak of the appreciation and admiration for my mom, Joyce Choate. You were a great teacher in the classroom and an even greater teacher outside the classroom in the arena of life. You have been a role model for me and instilled the values that are needed to get a project like this done. You motivated me when I needed it, listened to me whine, encouraged me, debated my word choices, and proof read every word of this book more than a few times! As with so many things in my life, I could not have done this without you.

## PUBLISHER'S ACKNOWLEDGMENTS

Corwin gratefully acknowledges the contributions of the following reviewers:

Glenda Ward Crawford
Professor of Education and
   Director of Teaching Fellows
Elon University
Elon, NC

Patti Grammens
Horizons Science Teacher and
   Science Department Chair
Lakeside Middle School
Cumming, GA

Katrina Ladopoulos
Teacher
Glendale Elementary, Madison
   Metropolitan School District
Madison, WI

Debra Las
Science Teacher
Rochester Public Schools ISD #535
Rochester, MN

Connie Molony
Reading Intervention Teacher
Carl Ben Eielson Middle School
Fargo, ND

Dr. Kathie F. Nunley
Educational Psychologist
Brains.org
Amherst, NH

# *About the Author*

**Jodi O'Meara** is a curriculum specialist for students with special needs and a professional developer for educators and administrators. She has presented at state, national, and international conferences. With over 15 years experience as a teacher and administrator of general education, special education, and gifted education, she recognizes the diverse needs of students and teachers. As early as 2002, Jodi's practices of successful differentiated instruction have been documented in multiple true accounts in *Chicken Soup for the Teacher's Soul* (Canfield & Hansen, 2002). Jodi specializes in professional development in the areas of differentiated instruction for students with special needs as well as students identified as gifted. She has also been involved with related projects and presentations such as response to intervention. Jodi was a cowriter of the Frameworks for Gifted Learners for the state of Florida as well as the Access Points, which align standards for students with significant disabilities to general education standards. She is a former president of the Florida Association for the Gifted and is on the board of directors for the Family Network on Disabilities in her local area. Additionally, Jodi is a certified life skills coach and provides guidance for leadership in business and education through her own company, Body and Mind Coaching and Consulting. Jodi believes that teachers can change the lives of people more effectively than any other professionals. She is strongly committed to supporting teachers in efforts to inspire their students.

# Introduction

## Overview

*If a man does not keep pace with his companions, perhaps it is because he hears a different drummer. Let him step to the music in which he hears, however measured or far away.*

—Henry David Thoreau

**D**ifferentiated instruction is certainly one of the most commonly used phrases in the field of education today. Every professional conference includes multiple sessions dealing with differentiated instruction. Educational vendors are sure to use this term to make the most of their marketing efforts. Differentiated instruction is frequently the topic of conversation at staff meetings and in teachers' lounges throughout the country. In fact, in a recent search on a popular search engine, when entering "differentiated instruction definition" more than 1,060,000 sites are found. Yet despite the frequency with which this term floats through educational discussions, there are still many unanswered questions related to the practice of differentiated instruction.

The term *differentiated instruction* has been around since the 1950s. It was commonly used to refer to providing individualized instruction delivered to meet the needs of each student. This commonly used term created the illusion that differentiated instruction and individualized instruction were one and the same. Unfortunately, this misconception still exists today and often intimidates teachers into thinking that they need to do 20 sets of lessons for each of the 20 students in the class. While individualized instruction is one aspect of differentiation, differentiated instruction offers more manageable and realistic approaches to reach the varied needs and strengths of students, and it also addresses the diversity in the classroom.

Carol Ann Tomlinson is considered by many to have promoted differentiated instruction and pushed it to the forefront of educational issues. Her definition is one of the most widely accepted today. She has defined differentiated instruction as a process in which a teacher proactively plans varied approaches to what students need to learn, how they will learn it, and how they can express what they have learned in order to increase the likelihood that each student will learn as much as he or she can as efficiently as possible (Tomlinson, 2003, p. 151).

Defining *differentiated instruction* is not the problem. In many cases, educators are provided with professional development that includes a definition and a description of what it looks like in practice. However, the most common question is still, How can I do it? There have been numerous studies conducted that show that even after receiving a great deal of training on differentiated instruction, most teachers are still not putting it into practice in the classroom. There may be a few different reasons for this. One reason may be that most of the emphasis has been placed on defining the concept and not applying it. Many publications and resources on the topic are often very philosophical or pedagogical in nature. This leaves many teachers able to talk about differentiated instruction yet still wondering how to do it. Differentiated instruction involves lifelong learning and can be very daunting. Educators may acquire a set of strategies to meet the needs of students by providing accommodations; however, this is only one piece of the puzzle. Teachers must be aware that there are multiple domains to consider for any one lesson. These considerations include the levels of complexity, degrees of abstraction, amounts of structure provided, degrees of student independence, and pace of learning, to name a few. Educators may often struggle to take each of these into account when planning or delivering lessons, and they end up overwhelmed.

Educators are looking for a way to put theory into practice. Differentiation is a process—not an event. Much of the work happens behind the scenes in the planning and preparation of instruction. Administrators observing teachers ask how they will know when they are seeing differentiated instruction during their observations. In many cases, there is no way to know if you are seeing it without a conversation about the practices and rationale involved in the instruction.

Differentiated instruction is not a singular, linear process. It is a flow chart with critical junctures and decisions. It is a process used in both planning and teaching. Most definitions agree that it is not just a philosophy but also a practice of meeting students' needs. Ideally, planning for differentiated instruction is best done in collaboration with a trusted colleague or group of professionals. The efforts of multiple people together can outweigh the efforts of each as individuals. Professional conversations can enhance the growth of each individual.

# PRINCIPLES OF DIFFERENTIATION

Differentiated instruction is responsive. A teacher who is differentiating instruction is responsive to the students and their needs as well as the context within which the students are learning. The best lesson in the world, with deep thinking required on the part of the students, is still not the best lesson if it occurs the period before a pep rally. The best lesson is one that takes into account the factors of the students and their environment. Differentiated instruction is student centered and therefore an organic, ever-changing process.

Differentiated instruction is based on assessment. Differentiated instruction requires knowledge of and response to the student in relation to the material being learned. Adjustments to instruction are made based on the way the student interacts with the material. Student assessment in any number of aspects related to learning is critical.

Differentiation requires a focus on the big picture as opposed to isolated skills. Differentiated instruction is more than providing accommodations, scaffolding, or pacing. It is the work that goes into the prelesson preparation as well as the ongoing and continuous response to the student's learning process. It goes beyond an acceptance of differences to an expectation of differences.

Differentiation requires an acceptance that everyone is not a master at everything and does not need to be. In all aspects of life, not everyone is as equally good at everything. Different people have different strengths and needs. In differentiated instruction, degrees of mastery of objectives must be established for each learner based on individual strengths and needs.

# WHAT THIS BOOK OFFERS

This book assumes that the reader has familiarity with the concept of differentiated instruction, even though there may be some variations in the individual's understanding of the concept. This book offers a process and a set of questions and considerations that can be used to put the definition into practice. It provides both the rationale and concrete steps to take on the practice of differentiated instruction—as a process rather than an event. It addresses the preplanning stages, planning, and implementation of instruction. It provides a concrete guide to be able to not only differentiate instruction but also communicate the rationale for instructional decisions made. Each aspect is based on research and is both conceptual and practical.

In order to begin the discussion of practice, there is a need for a discussion about knowledge and learning. The first part of the book, Chapters 1 and 2, combines both rationale and examples. This is necessary and provides the foundation and rationale for the process of differentiated instruction addressed in the rest of the book.

Do not flip through this book and go straight to the section on instructional strategies to see what new tools may be there. It is essential to read through the first chapter, which provides the foundation and frame of reference for the rest of the book. Without it, the definition of *differentiated instruction* will be as narrow as looking solely at best teaching practices in an isolated list.

This book is organized around a 10-step process of differentiated instruction. These steps are covered in the chapters of this book. Through each step listed in the process, Jen, a teacher practicing differentiated instruction, shares her thoughts, ideas, and practices. At the end of each chapter, the steps are listed with the step addressed within that chapter highlighted in bold. Following is this 10-step process:

Step 1: Examine standards and objectives to be taught. Determine the type of knowledge demanded of the standard and/or objective.

Step 2: Establish the conceptual understanding related to the facts and skills required.

Step 3: For any fact or skill, determine the level of fluency needed for mastery.

Step 4: Design independent student activities that address the facts and skills that are required, along with accommodations for students who need support in achieving mastery of the facts and skills.

Step 5: Reflect on personal knowledge and attitudes related to resources, the content, and the students.

Step 6: Preassess students in knowledge of facts, skills, conceptual understandings, experiences, attitudes, motivations, and ideas.

Step 7: Determine strategies for instruction at different levels of cognitive processing to include concrete, representational, and abstract processes.

Step 8: Determine the flow of classroom activities to include individual, small-group, and whole-group instruction.

Step 9: Determine benchmarks of student performance, and develop tools for ongoing measurement of progress.

Step 10: Develop selections and criteria for the summative product or performance that accurately reflect the intended outcomes of the unit.

## CHAPTER OVERVIEWS

Chapter 1 sets the stage so that subsequent chapters share not just what to do but how to do it. Differentiated instruction is less about the strategies of instruction and more about the levels of the learners as well as the levels of knowledge of the content being taught. Once there is a framework and systematic process to approach those two aspects of education, the implementation of instruction becomes manageable and systematic as well.

Chapter 2 addresses the issues of differentiated instruction in relation to standards. It builds on the types of knowledge discussed in Chapter 1 and describes the importance of using the standards as a platform from which to proceed. Chapter 2 discusses the compatibility and necessity of standards in differentiated instruction.

Chapter 3 examines the role of the foundational level of knowledge, which is composed of the facts and skills. This level of knowledge, defined in Chapter 1, must be addressed differently than other levels of knowledge. Chapter 3 discusses these differences and provides tools to address this level of knowledge.

Chapter 4 initiates the consideration of true self-reflection on the part of the teacher. The reflection includes areas of personal knowledge, attitudes toward the content, and attitudes toward the learners. There are guiding questions and a reflective tool for preparing to plan instruction.

Chapter 5 moves into the preplanning stages and considers both the fact-and-skill level of knowledge along with the conceptual level of knowledge in the role of preassessment. This chapter looks at multiple dimensions of learners and provides tools to assess students. It presents preassessment considerations that include the learner, as well as the context of the learning.

Chapter 6 contains the topics most commonly addressed in books on differentiated instruction. It provides a framework and a series of steps to take in planning for differentiated instruction. It includes instructional strategies. However, this chapter is different from most texts in that it addresses these topics in a related and systematic approach with a template to guide the process. This chapter provides not only the strategies but also the rationale for using specific strategies of instruction.

Chapter 7 continues the process of planning for differentiated instruction through the consideration of the management of instructional flow. This chapter includes topics of whole-group instruction, small-group instruction, as well as individualized instruction. It addresses the purpose as well as the strengths of and cautions for each model of delivery.

Chapter 8 addresses the process of continuous monitoring of students and their progress. This chapter includes assessing the physical and mental state of the learner, the context, and environment in which the learning is taking place, as well as student expectations. It includes the practices involved in implementing tiered instruction and accommodations. And, it addresses the relationship of differentiated instruction to response to intervention and instruction or RtI.

To complete the 10 steps, Chapter 9 provides information and ideas related to products, performance, and assessment. It provides guidelines for developing questions at the highest levels of knowledge and creating opportunities for authentic products and student performances.

Chapter 10 provides a look back as well as a look ahead. It addresses important issues, including the relationship between differentiated instruction and students identified as gifted or as having learning disabilities. It again brings forth RtI as a key partner in the differentiation process and philosophy.

Finally, at the end of the book in the appendix, there are templates, resources, and tools provided to assist with the processes of preplanning, planning, implementing, and reflecting with regard to differentiated instruction. Included is a set of questions for each chapter that lends itself to professional collaboration in the exploration of the concepts presented here. These questions can be used for a book study or other professional learning community. Each of the templates referred to in the chapters are provided as well.

# 1

## *Types of Knowledge*

*Information is not knowledge.*

—Albert Einstein

### Meet Jen

Jen is a teacher who has been teaching fifth grade for the last five years. She is proficient as a teacher. Her students and their parents have always been pleased with her teaching. Her administrator has also given her consistently high reviews. Jen has attended several workshops on the topic of differentiated instruction and is concerned about meeting the needs of each of the students in her class. Jen is looking forward to starting her sixth year of teaching and has new ideas to implement this year. She and the other fifth-grade teachers have some time for planning before the first day of school.

### Examining Knowledge

Jen and her team dive into their new science textbook eagerly. After thumbing through the text and related support materials, she begins her work by looking at the state standards and local standards she is required to address during the semester. During the first part of the year, she is focusing on physical science and must teach her students about states of matter. She reads the standard that says, "Students will identify three states of matter and recognize that changes in state can occur." Jen finds in the textbook where states of matter are addressed. There are two pages of reading and some basic questions at the end of the second page to focus on the identification of states of matter. The text provides pictures as well. Jen recognizes that the identification of states of matter means that students will simply name and define each state of matter. She also knows that to recognize the fact that changes can occur is fairly simple in nature. She wonders how her students will connect and relate to these standards.

Jen realizes that these standards are mostly a set of facts, and she needs to increase the level of understanding in order to provide a quality learning experience. She knows she must branch out beyond the textbook in order to make the learning meaningful. She asks herself, "Why is it important for students to know this?" and she determines that the real idea here is about states of matter being able to change when conditions change. She asks herself again why that idea is important for her students to learn and how it could apply to their lives. She thinks that she can take an approach or lens for these standards and teach her students the concept that outside factors influence and can create powerful change. She will use matter and states of matter as a way to promote student thinking about change on a broader level. She sees how this idea can connect to events in history, characterization in literature, mathematical functions, team sports in PE, and music history. She is satisfied that now she has something substantial with which to work.

Jen goes back to her standards along with the objectives in the textbook and begins to determine related facts and skills required to understand the standards along with the concepts of influence and change. She comes up with this list:

- There are four states of matter: solid, liquid, gas, and plasma.
- Temperature plays a role in determining states of matter.
- Combining matter can affect the state.
- Data collection is needed to document change.

Now, she can address each of these standards while focusing on the concept that outside factors influence and can create powerful change in multiple areas of life.

---

Jen shows us that all knowledge is not created equal. It is easy to get caught up in the content of the discipline and forget that there are different levels of knowledge or understanding required from standards. There is a hierarchy of knowledge that must be considered in order to differentiate instruction and prioritize both teaching and learning. There are distinct types of knowledge, and with the different levels or types comes different approaches to instruction.

## TABA'S CATEGORIES OF KNOWLEDGE

Early on, Hilda Taba (see Tomlinson, 2002) organized types of knowledge into categories. Her research became the basis for much of the more recent work done in the field of knowledge and learning. She identified five levels of knowledge:

1. Facts—a specific detail, which can be verified;

2. Skills—abilities, techniques, strategies, methods, or tools to utilize knowledge;

3. Concepts—a general idea or understanding, often a category or classification with common elements;

4. Principles—fundamental truths, laws, doctrines, or rules that explain the relationship between two or more concepts across topics or disciplines; and

5. Attitudes/dispositions—an intrapersonal reaction to new understandings involving a belief, appreciation, or value. (Tomlinson, 2002, p. 92)

Each of these types of knowledge has a role in learning and understanding. If we take these types of knowledge and put them into an inverted triangle, we can get a picture depicting levels of knowledge in an ordered way. (See Figure 1.1.)

**Figure 1.1**

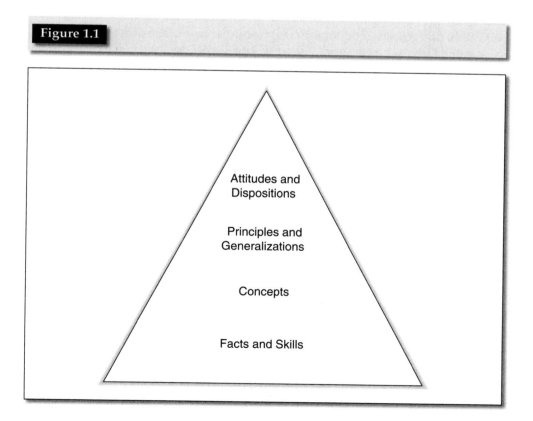

At the base of the triangle, facts and skills are placed together, although facts truly work as a foundation for skills in most cases. These are combined because they are, essentially, the foundation for understanding and application. In many instances, the facts and skills are the standards of a curriculum. They are the things we want students to know and do as a result of their learning. The teaching of the facts and skills is a very different process than teaching for conceptual understandings or other knowledge levels higher on the triangle.

## Facts and Skills as a Foundation

When a baby is very young, it learns what a cup is. The baby learns the fact that a cup is the object that provides a drink. The baby learns the word *cup*. The baby then learns how to use the cup. The baby learns that by bringing it to its mouth and tipping it, the baby gets what it wants. These two learning events often happen in conjunction with each other. Knowing a fact does little good if there is no knowledge of a skill to go with it. Ben Franklin stated that knowing some fact or how to do something was not as important as knowing how to make human kind better by utilizing that knowledge or skill. Facts and skills are interdependent.

In many cases, these are the types of knowledge with which educators begin instructional planning and complete the teaching process. The facts and skills are addressed, the students are assessed, and then the next fact or skill is addressed. The standards, in many cases, reinforce this process by emphasizing what students need to know and do. Teach, check for mastery, and move on. It is common to begin and end the learning process all within this foundational level.

## Conceptual Level of Knowledge

The next level of knowledge is the conceptual level. At this level, facts and skills are assimilated to create a concept. In some cases, standards are written at this level. In that case, the facts and skills are taught through direct instructional approaches, and then these facts and skills are brought together to create a concept. This is often a common sequence of the teaching process. Teaching for conceptual understandings requires different elements of consideration than the teaching of facts and skills.

After a baby knows what a cup is and can use a cup to drink, the baby begins to create a conceptual understanding. The baby learns that cups are different shapes, colors, and sizes. The baby may learn that different cups hold different liquids. As the baby develops a conceptual understanding, the baby recognizes that there are many cups that can provide what he or she wants to drink.

In the classroom, Jen may teach the fact that there are four common states of matter. Students will complete activities that transform liquids into different states of matter and label each state of matter attained. By learning the states of matter and completing activities transforming matter, the standards are accomplished. However, at the conceptual level, Jen's students will learn *why* changes in the states of matter occur. They will come to an understanding of what actually happens when heat is applied and why it causes a change in the state of matter. This is a conceptual understanding.

## Principles and Generalizations

After learning the concepts of temperature and its potential cause-effect relationship to states of matter, Jen's students will process the relationship between the matter and temperature at a new level. Students will take what they know about both states of matter and about temperature to create new understandings about change itself. Students will identify other cause-effect relationships to compare and contrast to the one involving the physics of temperature and states of matter. This is the creation of a principle that explains the relationship between concepts.

Only after a conceptual understanding is reached is knowledge at the principle level possible. This is the level in which learning becomes personalized. A learner creates his or her own principles based on conceptual understandings. Often, there is a blending of the creation of principles and generalizations. Once an understanding of the relationships between concepts has been achieved, it is human nature to seek other realms in which the knowledge will apply. Jen's students will explore how changes in matter may be like changes in weather conditions or even more far-reaching aspects, such as changes in politics or their own lives. Learning and teaching processes at this level and the next level are distinctly different than at other knowledge levels.

In the case of the baby with the cup, the baby will begin to realize that there are other containers besides cups that can provide a drink. The baby will experiment with multiple objects that hold liquids. The baby sees that bowls, watering cans, and buckets all hold water and can provide a drink. This learning goes beyond convergent thinking as the learner creates new truths through hypothesizing and making connections.

## Attitudes and Dispositions

Finally, the most personal level of learning is the level of attitudes and dispositions. At this level, the learning is internalized, processed, organized in a schema, and then evaluated. The learner makes decisions based on the knowledge. The learner determines his or her own level of interest or passion and level of motivation in further pursuing new questions. This level of knowledge is often overlooked or is not considered a category of knowledge. In Jen's classroom, she helps students internalize their knowledge by asking them to consider an influence that has changed a condition in their own lives and evaluate the significance of the influence at the time and compare it to the significance after the change occurred. Jen also has them complete an analogy to reflect the process of a change in matter in science class to this life event.

## Levels of Knowledge Is Not a Recipe

It is important to note here that although these levels are distinct knowledge levels, and are achieved through a specific developmental process, they do not need to be addressed in the classroom in the particular order in which they were presented here. Although facts and skills are a foundation to conceptual understandings, concepts can be approached first with facts and skills to follow. This approach creates a sense of exploration and prompts students to ask questions. In the case of Jen, she may have students first explore changes in matter on their own by providing them with materials to create changes. Students may discover, without knowing why, that heat can change matter. Later, she may explicitly teach the facts about the states of matter and the related facts, but she does not have to start instruction with the facts.

Each of these levels may not be addressed for every learner on every topic. There are several variables to consider, including interest and motivation on the part of the student as well as importance of the content. Generally, the first levels—facts and skills, along with concepts—are knowledge levels that all learners need, which is why they become the standard for all students. Many times, the levels of knowledge beyond concepts are not addressed.

In another example, I recently had a sprinkler system installed in my yard. After it was installed, the installer showed me where the sprinkler heads were in the lawn and flowerbeds. He showed me the timer and where the power source was. He gave me the basic facts. Then he showed me how to adjust the settings on the system and how to reset it if I needed to do so. I was able to perform the basic skills needed to operate the sprinkler system. I had the facts and skills needed to own the system.

Our conversation continued as he began to explain how the system should be monitored in the flowerbeds. He also showed me where water may be more likely to pool. At this point, he was combining facts and skills about irrigation, landscaping, and flora to create new concepts for me. This pushed my levels of both interest and ability. I was able to gain a conceptual understanding of the system's workings.

However, the conversation continued when the installer began sharing about the relationship of my sprinkler system to water-conservation efforts. He told me how my system was similar to and different from the local water treatment plant in its workings. He was now at the knowledge level involving principles. This was information that I did not need to know or have much desire to know. However, this installer was a specialist in irrigation. He had a reason and desire to reach this level of knowledge. Finally, he made a comment about how he was experimenting with his own personal irrigation system in order to create a better system. He was attempting to invent a new idea in the field of irrigation. Here, he displayed the highest level of knowledge, in which there is a contribution to a field of study. He was certainly at the highest level of knowledge, attitudes, and dispositions.

This example is important as it points out where the standards fall. It also illustrates that all learners do not have to reach all levels of knowledge for all content areas. It shows us that there is a level of proficiency that is considered a baseline. These are the standards of what all learners should know and do. Many times, these are within the knowledge levels of facts and skills, and concepts. This story also shows us that there are times when a learner wants or needs to go beyond the concepts to higher levels of knowledge. This recognition leads to the need for differentiated instruction.

## TYPES OF KNOWLEDGE AND DIFFERENTIATED INSTRUCTION

This triangle of knowledge is critical to understanding and is the basis for differentiated instruction. There is foundational knowledge, there are conceptual understandings, and there is specialized knowledge. There is a need to look at differentiation through at least three lenses. We need to consider meeting the needs of all learners with the understanding that all students need to master certain facts and skills. Therefore, the instruction and learning involved with facts and skills is a distinct process from the other levels. We need to also consider differentiation as we bring learners to the level of conceptual understandings so that the knowledge can be useful and transference can take place. This too becomes a distinct process of teaching and learning, different from facts and skills. Finally, we need to differentiate for learners who have the motivation and interest to go beyond the transfer process and enter deeper exploration. This third type of knowledge becomes the final distinct process and often involves very individualized instruction. (See Figure 1.2.)

It is equally important to note the language used here. Each of these three broadened levels of knowledge require different instructional approaches. *It is these distinct types of learning that should drive the instructional decisions and processes* (rather than the instructional processes driving the type of learning). This is the essence of differentiated instruction.

The differentiated practices educators implement is the instructional response to the levels of learning. The student's need for learning the facts and skills, concepts, and specialized knowledge determines the instructional

**Figure 1.2**

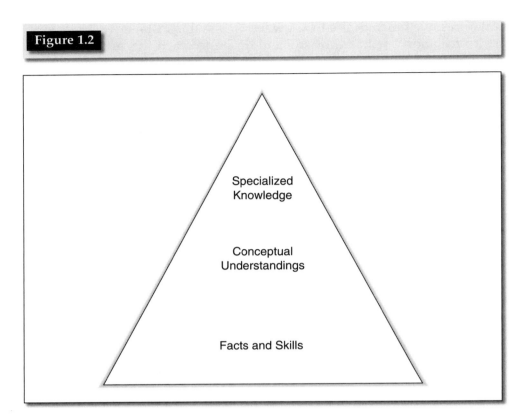

Specialized
Knowledge

Conceptual
Understandings

Facts and Skills

response. The decisions for instruction are made based on the student and the level of learning to be achieved. This is a significant shift in thinking. *We cannot start the teaching process with instructional practices. If we are going to implement differentiated instruction, we must start by identifying the knowledge levels and their relationship to the learners.* This is a very different approach than starting with the curriculum standards and simply addressing those in isolation. It is also different than the practice of implementing a research-based teaching strategy with no consideration being given to the content and how the student interacts with that content. This shift in thinking aligns to more recent practices of using Webb's hierarchy of depths of knowledge levels as opposed to older taxonomies (see Sullivan & Glanz, 2009).

This concept is of critical importance in thinking because this is the key to understanding how to differentiate instruction rather than what differentiated instruction is. Without clarity and consideration for this concept, there may be frustration in the implementation of differentiated instruction despite our having studied differentiated instruction or having learned teaching strategies such as tiered instruction or scaffolding. Differentiated instruction is often presented as being the practice of adjusting the content, the process, or the product. While that can be true, there needs to be consideration made for the level of knowledge being addressed. At the fact-and-skill level, there is little that can be done to adjust the content or the product, and yet there are unlimited numbers of ways to adjust the process. At the conceptual level, the process or product can more easily be differentiated while the content itself generally remains constant. It is at the top of the triangle, where principles and attitudes are situated, where all three elements, content, process, and product will be differentiated for learners. Without consideration for the type of knowledge as a desired learning outcome, standards may be compromised, instruction and assessment fall out of alignment, or differentiation becomes an unnatural fit with instruction and learning.

## SELF-APPLICATION

Professional development in the field of education has spent a great deal of effort on the foundational knowledge of differentiated instruction. Often, teachers are able to reflect mastery of the facts and skills related to differentiated instruction. These teachers, who receive professional development on the topic, in so many cases, understand the concept. But as educational professionals, teachers are thirsty to move toward the principles and disposition levels of their own knowledge. This is where authentic professional practice takes place. The support has been lacking at these levels because there has been a disconnect between instruction within professional development and these levels of learning. While there is a great deal of instruction occurring for teachers at the fact-and-skill level, there is little at the specialization level, which is the level at which many professionals in the field are seeking support.

## SUMMARY

There are different types of knowledge that require different approaches to teaching. Foundational knowledge is rooted in facts and skills. The conceptual level of understanding is based on the facts and skills but takes learning to a higher level. In designing instruction, this is the optimal place to initiate curriculum design. At the top tier of the levels of knowledge, there is a level that includes principles, generalizations, and attitudes and dispositions. This level of knowledge is specialized and specific to the learner and the content. It is addressed by need or desire rather than as part of a standard curriculum. Each of these three main levels of knowledge is approached differently in the differentiation of instruction.

# 2

## *Moving Beyond Foundational Knowledge*

*Educating is not the filling of a pail but the lighting of a fire.*

—William Butler Yeats

When educators are discussing curriculum, the term *standards-based curriculum* is often used. This means that the standards are used to drive instruction. It is generally required that standards be taught in the educational system. Standards ensure that all students receive the foundations of learning needed. Standards are, in essence, the baseline of what all students should know and be able to do. Standards provide consistency and a bar for levels of achievement. Well-written standards also provide a systematic, ordered framework from which to present instruction. They function as the road map for instruction.

It is important to examine the standard being addressed to determine the level of learning into which the standard falls. This is important to identify up front because it impacts differentiated instruction tremendously. By identifying the level of knowledge in which the standard falls, an educator can begin to think about how to approach the standard in the instructional process. The approach to instruction and the learning process is different for facts and skills than it is for concepts.

# CONCEPTUAL KNOWLEDGE AS A START

With the emphasis on standards-based instruction, educators often begin with the standard and plan a lesson or series of lessons around that standard or objective. Frequently, the process follows a pattern of first teaching the related facts and skills which lead up to conceptual understanding. The lesson or series of lessons then concludes with how the facts and skills are related to each other and the concept is presented. In some cases, instruction falls short and stops at the mastery of the isolated facts and skills and never reaches any conceptual knowledge.

There is no rule that says this needs to be the progression, however, and in considering differentiated instruction, it may not always be the best process. In most cases, it is more advantageous to consider the conceptual level of knowledge before the fact-and-skill level. Beginning the instructional process with a conceptual understanding allows the learner to make connections with the facts and skills upon which the concept is based, as well as stretch toward creating personal theories and generalizations.

## Jen's Work With Changing
## From Facts and Skills to Concepts

When Jen started teaching, she required each of her students to memorize a poem by a particular writer. She had some students who could do this very easily while others struggled with the memorization. After having this requirement for a year or two, Jen was asked why students had to do this and what were the students really learning in the process. She realized she never questioned what the purpose was. She was doing it because her own teacher had required it of her as a student, and she had enjoyed it. She had also found a way to link the activity to a poetry standard within the literature strand. After thinking about the purpose, she realized that her intent was for her students to discover and experience the rhythm within poetry. The following year, she changed her approach. She focused her efforts on teaching her students about the rhythm in poetry and in other forms of writing rather than focusing on the memorization of a work. Instead of having to memorize a poem from the writer that Jen liked best, she assigned students to choose a poem or song that the student felt reflected the concepts of rhythm she had taught.

By changing her approach to focus on the concept rather than on the skill of memorizing a poem, students gained a greater understanding of poetry and Jen was able to potentially differentiate both her instruction and the student product itself.

This change in Jen's thinking and teaching is a reflection of her studies of the Understanding by Design Framework by Grant Wiggins and Jay McTighe (1998). They call this aspect of the curriculum design approach *discovering the big idea.* This approach encourages educators to ask why the fact or skill is necessary in the first place as they plan instruction. That usually becomes the big idea that drives the planning of instruction. By doing so, doors for possibilities to differentiate instruction also open.

## MOVING TOWARD CONCEPT-BASED STANDARDS AND KNOWLEDGE LEVELS

A common benchmark in language arts indicates that "the student will know commonly used abbreviations." This is clearly factual knowledge and falls at the foundational level. While important, this is a very limiting standard. There is very little range of criteria with a standard such as this. There are only two ways an educator can address facts and skills because they are black and white. A student knows it or does not know it. This limits an educator to only one of two instructional approaches. The teacher can use drill and practice so that the fact or process becomes fluent, or the teacher can instruct the student on a way to generate the fact or skill within a short response time using accommodations or supports. For instance, the multiplication tables are facts. They can either be memorized, or a learner can develop strategies to reference the facts in a quick way. Instruction becomes limited and learning is restricted. If, however, we move the starting point of the instructional approach to the conceptual level of knowledge, as we saw Jen do, we have many possibilities for instruction.

## WHY NOT FOCUS ON JUST THE FACTS AND SKILLS?

As stated earlier, traditionally, the instructional process has started with the teaching of facts and skills followed by a progression toward conceptual understanding. Many times, however, instruction never reaches that far. Due to time constraints, standardized testing pressures, or expectations to cover material within a course, learning is often a series of facts and skills to be mastered, checked off like a to-do list.

There are several reasons why it is best not to focus instruction solely on the level of fact- and skill-based knowledge even when the standard is written as a fact or skill. Following are some reasons why instruction should always be rich enough to include a conceptual understanding.

### 1. There is a lack of transfer.

Students learn facts and skills in isolation and cannot apply them to other situations. A kindergarten child was at the beach with her grandmother and they picked up shells. The grandmother said to the girl, "I have a shell and you have two shells. How many do we have altogether?" The little girl replied that she did not know and the grandmother provided encouragement. The grandmother said, "Honey, you know how to add. What is one plus two?" and the little girl said. "I don't know. I only know how to do it with ducks and kittens."

Hopefully, the conceptual understanding will come for her later. However, this reflects the result of focusing on the skill of adding rather than the concept of addition. This may seem like a slight difference, but the implications are huge.

### 2. There is a lack of understanding.

If you ask a person how to divide fractions, he or she is likely to tell you to take the reciprocal of the second fraction and then multiply the fractions. When you ask most people why that is, most have no idea. "It just works" is the most common response. So, this is a great skill if you have a worksheet of problems with fractions to divide. A group of teachers were asked, "When is the last time you used the skill of dividing fractions?" After a bit of pondering, one teacher said she did when she cooked. She took half the amount stated on a recipe to make half the number of servings. This is a teacher who teaches fractions yet she just described the process of multiplying fractions, not dividing them. This teacher, like many, is a product of an educational system that focused on facts and skills rather than conceptual understandings. In this example, there is no clear understanding on the concept of the division of fractions. This leads to problems with both application and transfer.

### 3. There is a lack of meaning, emotion, or motivation attached.

In fifth grade, I was required to memorize 36 prepositions in alphabetical order. I sang them to the tune of Yankee Doodle and got them correct on my exam. However, it was not until seventh grade that I knew what a preposition was. From fifth grade until seventh, there was no meaning for me and this resulted in little motivation for me to retain the prepositions for a period of time longer than the exam. I really did not care what a preposition was because it held no meaning for me.

### 4. Facts and skills in isolation are not real to life.

To learn facts and skills without having a conceptual understanding is superficial. It is something done on worksheets but not in real life. People learn in context. The human brain searches for meaning when something new is presented and connections are constantly sought. If the words "Biggler is a Dartibough" are presented as new vocabulary words, the brain instantly tries to connect what a Biggler or a Dartibough could be in relation to something already known. The brain searches past experiences, similarities to known words, or words of similar structure in attempt to make sense of the words. This is a natural process in the brain. Memorizing facts in isolation serves little purpose without a context.

### 5. Facts and skills can be most difficult for struggling learners.

Many students who struggle the most academically are those who have processing deficits. These are students with identified auditory or visual processing problems. Some have difficulties with receptive language and others with expressive language. Another large group of struggling learners is students who do not speak English as a first language. These students also often struggle with language. For students in these groups, the most difficult tasks for them to complete are often those dependent on regurgitating facts. Some of these students are very bright and have high levels of understanding. These students often are making connections and creating thoughts at the generalization level of knowledge. However, the task of identifying a particular fact, vocabulary term, or other fact-based level of knowledge out of context can be extremely difficult. In teaching these students, starting instruction at the facts-and-skills level of knowledge is often limiting and discouraging for these learners.

### 6. Facts and skills alone will not help students perform well on standardized testing.

For all of the reasons listed above, the focus on facts and skills alone will not allow the student to transfer knowledge and do well on testing. This is more of a by-product than a viable reason to start with conceptual knowledge—rather than at the facts-and-skills level—but it is worth mentioning. With all the pressures of high-stakes testing, there are often concerns about students being prepared to do well on the tests. By teaching to the level of knowledge of facts and skills, the student is often unable to successfully complete questions and problems presented in a way that varies at all from the way it was taught in the classroom.

Therefore, while it is important and even essential for students to have mastered facts and skills to established levels of fluency and accuracy, it is also important that the conceptual knowledge be the focus for the instructional process. By approaching the standards through the hierarchy of levels of knowledge, one can identify the types of standards as being facts-or-skills knowledge or conceptual knowledge. For these different levels of knowledge, differentiated instruction must be approached differently. At the facts-and-skills foundational level, differentiation primarily involves providing supports and additional strategies to master the content. Differentiation of facts and skills will be addressed in greater depth in Chapter 3.

As the learning moves into the conceptual level, however, there are many opportunities for differentiating the content, the process, and the product. To move foundational objectives to higher levels of knowledge, an examination of why the fact or skill is necessary provides direction toward the conceptual understandings. Conceptual knowledge allows the learner to create meaning and allows for application of the knowledge to take place.

At the end of each chapter, a list of the 10 steps of differentiated instructional planning will be provided. With each chapter, this process grows. This chapter has covered the first two essential steps in differentiating instruction.

# DIFFERENTIATED INSTRUCTION: THE 10-STEP PROCESS

**Step 1: Examine standards and objectives to be taught. Determine the type of knowledge demanded of the standard and/or objective.**

**Step 2: Establish the conceptual understanding related to the facts and skills required.**

Step 3: For any fact or skill, determine the level of fluency needed for mastery.

Step 4: Design independent student activities that address the facts and skills that are required, along with accommodations for students who need support in achieving mastery of the facts and skills.

Step 5: Reflect on personal knowledge and attitudes related to resources, the content, and the students.

Step 6: Preassess students in knowledge of facts, skills, conceptual understandings, experiences, attitudes, motivations, and ideas.

Step 7: Determine strategies for instruction at different levels of cognitive processing to include concrete, representational, and abstract processes.

Step 8: Determine the flow of classroom activities to include individual, small-group, and whole-group instruction.

Step 9: Determine benchmarks of student performance, and develop tools for ongoing measurement of progress.

Step 10: Develop selections and criteria for the summative product or performance that accurately reflect the intended outcomes of the unit.

# SUMMARY

While facts and skills are foundational knowledge and necessary for mastering standards, facts and skills often fail to promote true understanding. When facts and skills are the focus of learning and not coupled with conceptual knowledge, the learner often finds the learning to be of little meaning or use. Fact-and-skill–based knowledge can be linked to conceptually based knowledge by asking why the facts and skills are necessary for a student to master. By asking why, the big idea or conceptual understanding is often uncovered. This conceptual knowledge needed by the learner should be the primary focus of instructional planning—as opposed to simply facts and skills in isolation.

# 3

# *Differentiation of Foundational Knowledge*

*The only trouble with facts is that there are so many of them.*

—Samuel McChord Crothers, essayist

In the previous chapter, it was established that facts and skills are the foundational level of knowledge. Although learning ideally begins at the conceptual level and branches out to facts and skills as well as principles and generalizations, the facts and skills of the foundational level have a critical role in the learning process. While the foundational skills and facts must be learned, they should not be the end goal for student learning. At this level, differentiation involves assessment-based decisions that support students by providing accommodations in the area of processing. Additional time, different approaches to learning, and restructured order of learning are some of the types of accommodations that are effective for students in learning facts and skills.

# APPROACH TO INSTRUCTION AT THE FACT-AND-SKILL LEVEL

Despite their importance, facts and skills should not be the starting or stopping point. Classroom instructional time is too valuable. For the most part, the practice and repetition required for mastery of facts and skills should be planned as independent practice rather than instructional time. This level of knowledge is geared toward gaining competence in memorization and fluent production. It is based on practice and drill. Differentiation of the independent practice is based on the student's ability to accurately perform the skill well.

There are times, however, when it is appropriate and necessary to provide direct instruction of the facts and skills. Before practice and reinforcement can occur, a student must receive instruction in order to be practicing accurate facts and processes. There are only two possible initial approaches to instruction related to the mastery of facts and skills. The first approach is for the learner to be exposed to a fact enough times so that it becomes memorized. It is then stored in permanent or long-term memory. This memorization process allows for a learner to develop a base on which to place other forms of thinking and knowledge. The fact must be able to be accessed and referred to easily and efficiently. Common facts at the level of mastery required for long-term memory are those that are most familiar to us. It may be our parents' names, our address, or a fact needed for us to function throughout the day. It can also be something that captured our interest or is related to an emotion on some level. Throughout the learning process, there are many facts required for mastery in any particular content area. A command of multiplication tables is a simple, common example of required facts to be mastered.

The second way to address a fact in the instructional process is to teach a strategy to gain quick or easy access to the fact. If a fact cannot be mastered to the point of being automatic, instruction may be needed to focus on a strategy to access the fact efficiently and accurately. Instructional decisions at the foundational level involve determining the degree of fluency required and the level of accurate production of the fact or skill.

# FLUENCY AND AUTOMATICITY OF FACTS AND SKILLS

Once it has been determined that students must master a certain fact or skill, the educator must then consider the importance of automaticity of the skill. Automaticity refers to the ability to recall a fact without having to rely on cognitive processes used for problem solving. It is the ability to recall automatically. Some facts and skills need to be in the automatic long-term memory for instant retrieval in order to function effectively. For instance, a secondary-level math teacher may determine that students must know multiplication tables with complete automaticity so that more complex math can be addressed. In this case, the level of fluency with the facts and skills is critical. A history teacher may find it just as important for students to know the capitals of European countries, however, fluent recognition rather than fluent generation may be more critical. The question becomes, what does mastery look like for a particular fact? Is it necessary for the facts or skills to be instantly generated? Is there the leeway for recall within a short wait-time? What is an acceptable amount of processing time in order to still remain efficient?

Fluency is dependent on the ability to store information in long-term memory for efficient retrieval. The brain takes in numerous bits of information simultaneously all the time. The brain constantly filters the information to determine the relevant information from the irrelevant information. The brain functions in this way because the relevant information, at this point, goes into what is called *working memory*. Working memory can hold up to about seven bits of information at any one time. The working memory deals with these bits of information in order to make sense of the input. The brain searches for connections and meaning while processing the information. The more complex or unfamiliar the bits of information are that come into the brain, the more "brainpower" it takes to make sense of it.

As the brain receives input and determines a fact to be relevant, it will create links between what is currently in the brain and the new information. For example, when hearing the name of a person, the brain searches for the relationship with that person. The brain goes through its folders like a search engine. Where have I heard that name before? What relationship does that name have to me? What context has that name been used in? What emotions are related to that name? The brain even has an advanced search option when needed. If the brain cannot make the connection to identify the name, it will process it in relation to what it does have for possible connections. It will search for names that sound like that name or search for other names in what may be the same context that the name could be found.

However, as the brain continues to receive a familiar bit of information or the same information repeatedly, the pathways in the brain start creating a direct link to the meaning or process related to that information. For instance, when you hear your own name being called, there is much less processing in order to recognize it as your name. You hear your name and the brain reacts instantly. A deep pathway has been made through much repetition so that it does not need to perform a search in order to recognize your own name. This automaticity frees up space in the working memory in order to process other information. With the average capacity of processing being about seven bits at a time, recognizing your own name can be done without having to take up one of those seven bits of brainpower.

# INSTRUCTIONAL PROCESS OF TEACHING FACTS AND SKILLS

Initial instruction of facts and skills is usually done through direct instruction and modeling. The principles of gradual release of responsibility come into play for instruction that is skill based. In this instance, instruction starts with the teacher doing the majority of the work and modeling for students. The modeling should include think-aloud or metacognitive strategies so that the students observe the process. Then the students attempt the skill while being closely guided and coached. In some cases, the skill is completed together by both the learner and instructor. When competence and confidence are achieved through this process, students take on the responsibility of the skill and work to complete it independently. Supports are put in place throughout this process to be sure the student is learning the fact or skill correctly.

Differentiation takes place in the form of scaffolding. This involves the amount of guidance and support provided for a student in the learning process. A student who is lacking either skills or confidence may need more time on the guided practice, and a student who learns quickly may need very little time with supports in place. The movement through this gradual release of responsibility is dependent on the student's ability and rate of learning.

After this direct instructional stage, the student assumes responsibility for the fact or skill, and the learning process becomes one to increase fluency and accuracy. This is done through practice and repetition. It can be done independently and does not require instructional time. Differentiated instruction may include adjusting the amount of time or number of repetitions a student performs within the practice.

## Jen's Initial Instruction

Jen's learning objective indicates that students will add fractions with unlike denominators. She first surveys the students' abilities with fractions by using a gamelike activity where student have to add fractions with like denominators and recognize fractions paired with their pictures in sets. This provides Jen with information regarding the background skills and subskills needed to add fractions. Jen also provides two prompts asking students to calculate the sum of two fractions with unlike denominators. Jen discovers that while the background and subskills are in place for all but four students, only two show the ability to add fractions with unlike denominators.

Jen starts with small group instruction provided for remediation for the four students who do not have the skills in place to add fractions with like denominators or pair fractions with pictures. This occurs while other students are working independently on identifying common multiples of sets of numbers. Jen finishes with the small group and goes back to teaching the whole group. She introduces adding fractions with unlike denominators and models the process using metacognitive, or think-aloud, strategies and visual supports. After her initial instruction, she has all students complete another fact together following her lead. She does this one more time and then tells students that they can try one on their own. While they are not actually on their own, Jen works her way around the room coaching and guiding students through the process.

Jen identifies some students who need more supports and modeled examples. She also finds some who can complete the task independently with very little coaching. Jen allows those students to move on to complete an independent activity while she goes back to an increased level of support with the others. She models and uses a think-aloud strategy to work through another problem. She then asks students to try again while she provides support and guidance to the students. These students may need several practices at this stage with the guidance and support before being ready for an independent try. There are also students who need more modeling and examples before approaching the task. Jen provides these students with support in the form of increased scaffolding to help them achieve success.

## ASSESSMENT OF FLUENCY AND ACCURACY

During this instructional process, assessments focus on both accuracy and rate of fluency. It is not enough to identify if the student can get to the correct answer. When talking about mastery of facts and skills that are essential, it is important to know if the facts are part of long-term memory or if the facts require processing, working memory, or brainpower. It is important to assess both fluency as well as accuracy. Therefore, the assessment of facts for mastery should have time constraints.

This is not to say that one-minute quizzes are always appropriate. In fact, that can often put undue stress on a student who may then get flustered and become panicked. In times of panic, the thought processes can shut down so that a person functions in a primitive survival mode. Performance may suffer in both fluency and accuracy. Research has shown for several years that even on an IQ test, the performance of a person under stress is generally lower than the performance of that same person without high stress. Instead of administering an assessment in which students must complete as much of a task as possible within a short time frame, it makes more sense to have students complete a designated number of tasks and note the amount of time that it took each student to complete the tasks. The shift here allows for an experience of success and accomplishment for students rather than setting them up to be unable to complete tasks presented. Generally, the only students who enjoy the timed quizzes are those who are successful and complete the tasks within the time limit. Other students often feel a sense of failure. So, while time is a critical element, it can be measured through different approaches.

## INFORMAL MEASURES OF FLUENCY AND ACCURACY

Instead of timed tests, informal measures may sometimes be more appropriate. One strategy is to use response boards. Response boards require all students to respond to a prompt or question by indicating an answer on a board or card and holding up the board. This strategy is not only a good way to assess fluency of facts and skills but also a good management strategy. It increases the amount of time on task for students since all students are required to answer. Research presented by William Heward (1990) shows that using response cards instead of hand-raising for 30 minutes a day increases student responses by about 3,700 additional responses in one year.

Response cards can take the form of wipe-off boards, index cards, or colored papers. They can be very easy to manage, reuse, and create. For example, a green card held up could indicate agreement as "yes," "true," or "agree." A red card held up may indicate disagreement as "no," "false," or "disagree." A teacher can then make a simple statement and have students hold up a card in response. A single card could have a number one on one side and a number two on the other. The teacher can provide two choices and students hold up either a one or a two to indicate their answer. When using white boards or wipe-off boards, which can be made quite inexpensively from laminated card stock or shower board tiles, the response possibilities become open ended. Students can write a word, number, or any simple response on the board and hold it up.

For those who are fortunate enough to have technology available, the use of audience response systems or "clickers" as they are commonly known are a fantastic upgrade on response cards. These clickers allow the teacher to quickly collect, organize, and sort data and motivate the students as well.

The day after Jen introduced adding fractions with her initial lesson, she initiated an assessment to indicate the levels of mastery of her students. Jen used her classroom response system and observed student responses, looking for both accuracy as well as fluency. In this case, fluency was indicated by the rate at which the calculation was being done and the students clicked in to respond. By doing this, Jen found that two of her students were not getting correct answers or calculations, while two different students never answered any questions incorrectly. The rest of her class fell between those two ends. Jen was able to sort her students into three groups for the purpose of providing supports at different levels so that each could become fluent and accurate at computing the addition of fractions with unlike denominators.

## DIFFERENTIATION BASED ON ASSESSMENT OF FLUENCY AND ACCURACY

The purpose of preassessment is to gather information in order to drive instruction. Therefore, the educator needs to be collecting data while response cards or any other assessments are implemented. Preprinted cards with students' names on them may be used by just sorting names based on performance. Data should provide student information to place them into one of three categories. Students with apparent mastery and fluency are sorted into one group. Students with correct answers who are lacking fluency are sorted into a second group. Students lacking both fluency and accuracy are sorted into a third group.

In response to this information, there is one group who needs no instructional time on facts and skills. There are two groups with needs that must be addressed. The second group, who had good accuracy but weak fluency, should be given ample practice and repetition to master the facts and skills. In some cases, students may not have had the opportunity to practice; with focused practice, these students may achieve mastery with fluency. Because they're accurate but not fluent, they are good candidates for partner practice. Pairing these students with others from this same group is an effective way to increase and reinforce the skills and facts. The third group of students, who need immediate instructional attention, is the group lacking accuracy. These students must be provided with some direct, corrective instruction. It does them no good to practice and repeat inaccurate information. It will do harm to have them practice and repeat incorrect facts or skills. These students must first become accurate before moving toward the practice and repetition being done by the second group.

In Jen's situation, she will provide interventions and reteaching for one group. The second group will use software products and peer activities to work toward mastery, while the third group will be provided with enrichment opportunities.

Following is Figure 3.1, which reflects differentiated instruction with regards to the facts and skills as a foundation to conceptual understandings.

**Figure 3.1**  The Decision-Making Process for the Instruction of Facts and Skills

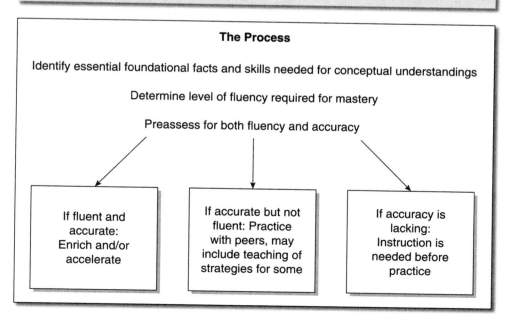

**The Process**

Identify essential foundational facts and skills needed for conceptual understandings

Determine level of fluency required for mastery

Preassess for both fluency and accuracy

| If fluent and accurate: Enrich and/or accelerate | If accurate but not fluent: Practice with peers, may include teaching of strategies for some | If accuracy is lacking: Instruction is needed before practice |

## TOOLS AND TECHNOLOGY FOR
## FACT- AND SKILL-BASED ACQUISITION

There are many strategies and tools for practice and repetition available. These include but are not limited to practice such as flashcards, column note taking for studying, repeated readings or recordings, practiced readings, and audience-response systems. There are many software programs in the areas of reading and mathematics that also provide excellent vehicles for repetition and fluency practice. Each of these can provide systematic repetition and, in some cases, efficient data collection and organization. In each of these types of practice, the learner is the one responsible for mastery of facts.

## ACCOMMODATIONS AFFORDED
## WITH FACTS AND SKILLS

In some cases, however, a learner cannot reach mastery on the automaticity of facts. There are a number of reasons for this. Learning disabilities may make it difficult for the brain to create the direct links for instantaneous recall. In addition, all of us have had the experience of not being able to remember a fact even through repetition and practice. People's names, a friend's birth date, a particular brand of a product are often the facts that frustrate us as adults. For whatever reason, there are some learners and some facts that create difficulties when they are put together. For these learners, facts need to be addressed differently. In this case, differentiated instruction is needed, and the learner is not yet ready for independent practice.

When considering multiplication tables in mathematics, it is generally accepted that students must learn these facts to the point of automaticity. This is needed so that the brain is available to process other information in solving problems. If there are only about seven bits that the brain can process at any one time, the desire is for the math fact to not take up one of those spaces in working memory. However, sometimes students struggle with getting these facts into the brain where they can be efficiently and effectively accessed. This is when instruction is required to teach a strategy to get access to the fact without relying on long-term memorization or rapid retrieval of the fact.

This is a different approach because it does require the occupation of space in the working memory in the brain. Processing strategies must be both quick and accurate for students to benefit. One example of a strategy such as this is using fingers to learn the nines times tables. By counting over from left to right on the fingers, and then putting down the finger of the second multiple, the left side indicates the number of tens and the right side indicates the number of ones, to create the product.

Strategies like these should be taught only if the facts and skills cannot be established in long-term memory through regular practice and repetition. First of all, it is a slower process to use such strategies. Secondly, it does not contribute toward the acquisition of conceptual understandings. Finally, it continues to take up working memory—just for a shorter period of time than without a strategy. This often makes the skill or fact functional, as opposed to one at a level of mastery. However, being functional at a skill or fact is certainly better than lacking accuracy or lacking a strategy to get an accurate answer.

These strategies that help struggling students may include the use of pneumonic devices. They may include pencil-and-paper strategies. Creating lists and reminders are such strategies. In order to determine the most appropriate strategy, it is important to ask why a fact or skill is important. If we go back to the standard, "the student will write the numbers from 1–50" it is essential to know why that skill is being addressed before instruction, supports for learning, or assessment can take place. If the standard is to see if the student can write numbers, then the amount of numbers can be reduced but the teacher should not allow for the student to say—and not *write*—the numbers. If the purpose is to see if the student knows the numbers in consecutive order, then orally reciting them would be fine, but writing them out of order or randomly on a paper would not be acceptable. If the objective is to see if the student understands the patterns involved in base 10 then the teacher could have the student use a computer to type them or allow him to show the patterns using manipulatives, but the teacher could not group the objects for the student. Without clarity as to why a standard is being taught, it becomes impossible to systematically provide instruction and supports.

Accommodations can be provided through different means. The accommodations provided are different for facts and skills than for conceptual understandings. The tools that support the learner in executing a process or organizing the learner's ideas allow for performance rather than understanding. Accommodations can be provided in multiple formats. The degree to which the accommodations are provided can also be considered as an area of differentiation. On the following page is a chart (Figure 3.2) of different accommodations in the three formats of materials, processing, and assignments or products.

At the level of facts and skills, the use of manipulatives commonly provides supports for the learning process by making the process concrete. Manipulatives and tools assist the learner in completing skills or obtaining accurate facts efficiently. These may include tools in reading, such as pointers or bookmarks. In math this includes counting blocks, base-10 blocks, and other tangible items. In learning the order of the planets, a student may need to move the plastic replications of the planets to arrange them in the proper order. Other hands-on strategies include the use of tools. This includes reference materials and calculators. For the purposes of practice

**Figure 3.2**

| Materials: | |
|---|---|
| Manipulatives | Concrete objects used to promote visualization and exploration |
| Software | Computer programs that provide repetitions and systematic practice |
| Tools | Includes references, calculators, rulers, highlighters—used to assist in an area not related to the objective being assessed—for instance spell-check access may be a tool if the objective involves the writing process or an activity in which spelling is not the focus |
| Self-correcting tools | Includes such things as computer software games, center activities with answers found nearby—provides accurate practice and builds confidence |
| **Processing:** | |
| Pneumonic devices and other linguistic strategies | Provides auditory strategies for memorization |
| Visuals and pictures | Includes symbols and printed cues designed to provide representations to remind or call attention to a direction, process, or idea |
| Graphic organizers | Provides representations to organize thoughts and ideas |
| Charts and lists | Provides support in memorization |
| "Tricks" | Includes "short-cuts" and strategies for accuracy—used to provide a method to obtain accurate responses |
| Supports for modeling and guidance | Provides models for reference and assistance to complete skills accurately |
| **Assignments/Products:** | |
| Length of assignment | Shorten assignment for students who work more slowly |
| Time allowed to completion | Provides extended time to complete work |
| Supports for guidance | Provides assistance to a student so that the experience is successful |
| Visually adjusted tasks | Provides visual assurance and organization and provides less reading—the prompt with more words is on the left and the term with fewer words is on the right |

and repetition, software and self-correcting games also open an avenue for differentiation by the degree to which they are used by a student.

At the processing stages, graphic representations and graphic organizers are other tools that can support a learner struggling with the mastery of facts and skills. Graphic representations are often tools students learn to use through direct instruction. They are a way to replace a student's dependence on manipulatives and concrete objects. Rather than actual objects, the learner may rely on tally marks, lists, or processing outlines to maintain accuracy. Two examples of this type of accommodation is the use of a list to remember items to buy at the grocery store or a set of tally marks to help a student count numbers when adding. At a more complex level of usage, these tools may involve the use of picture symbols or icons that have personal meaning for a student. In learning the order of the planets, a student may rely on the picture of the planets depicted in order on a poster.

Another type of accommodation for students struggling in the process of mastering facts and skills is abstract or linguistic in nature. These strategies may include a song that states a process, a pneumonic device, or an auditory cue. The television special programming of *School House Rock* capitalized on this, and many adults can sing the songs about interjections, conjunctions, and adverbs. In another example, a student may learn that anytime he hears the words "less than" he should subtract numbers. This reliance on cues is more abstract than the other types of accommodations and not always accurate, as reflected in the example with subtraction. However, these strategies students learn can be very helpful as an initial approach to a challenge.

Finally, at the processing level, the student may learn tricks or short cuts to get correct answers. An example of this strategy includes learning the number of days in a month by counting their knuckles and spaces between the knuckles. When these types of strategies are taught, it is important to consider the ability of the student to execute the trick in a variety of situations and the ease of which it is executed. It is also important to focus a great deal of attention on conceptual understanding for that student, as he or she will lack the use of alternative strategies if needed.

## ADDRESSING STUDENTS AT MASTERY LEVEL WITH FACTS AND SKILLS

Little has been said about the group of students who have mastery of facts and skills with both fluency and accuracy. The terms *enrich* and *accelerate* are very broad terms. The idea is that these students should not be spending all their time practicing skills and facts already mastered. That leads to boredom and frustration. They should also not be required to do extra work or be used to lead practice and reinforcement drills for peers. These students should be provided respectful tasks that challenge them at their level. Sandra Kaplan provides a wonderful chart (see Figure 3.3) illustrating depth and complexity that can be used to guide enrichment for these students. When creating learning experiences for students, this chart offers elements to add to the depth and complexity of the content. This chart can be used to help create questions and learning activities to challenge students at the highest performance levels for any content.

If there are students who have a mastery of the facts, they need to be challenged at the highest levels of the types of knowledge. These students should be provided with activities and instruction that require them to apply the facts and skills to create concepts and theories and make hypotheses. The chart (Figure 3.3) is one tool that can be used to bring the levels of knowledge to an elevated point. The focus of the instruction by the educator will be approached at the conceptual level. However, these students may approach the content starting with the creation of their own ideas and theories. The theories can then later be proved or disproved through formal instruction.

Although facts and skills are the foundation for other levels of knowledge, they need not be the starting point in instruction. They also cannot be the stopping point. The focus must be on the conceptual understanding while encouraging and enabling the facts and skills to be mastered. This is in opposition to focusing on learning all the facts and skills and then, after mastery, pulling them all together for conceptual understanding.

---

## Last Thoughts on Jen

After assessing students' responses to the initial instruction, Jen created three groups of students. One of those groups needed reteaching and interventions, while another group needed enrichment. Jen created small groups on the basis of those needs. In the group with struggling learners, Jen found that many of them simply needed additional instruction, reminders, or some background vocabulary terms. There were, however, a few who continued to struggle with the skill. For those students, Jen provided accommodations based on their needs. She provided fraction bars for these students as well as some problems with their answers while she guided and coached them as they worked. Jen also used accommodations to adjust for the third group, who had already mastered the skill of adding fractions with unlike denominators. Those students were assigned additional complexity by being asked to explore how the process of addition involving mixed numbers would be the same or different than the process using only fractional parts. The connections between the skills increase the levels of complexity for these students.

---

| Figure 3.3 | Elements of Depth and Complexity |

| Trait | Descriptor | Example |
|---|---|---|
| Details | The attributes, traits, and characteristics that define and distinguish the topic | An investigation of what makes a beagle different than a hound dog |
| Patterns | The order, repetition, and predictability of an occurrence | A study of the Earth's temperature over the past millennium |
| Trends | The ongoing, external influences related to the topic | A study of the economy as influenced by war and peace |
| Unanswered Questions | The professional mysteries and ambiguities that remain unresolved surrounding a topic | A study of how ancient civilizations far across the globe had so many similarities in culture and technologies |
| Rules | The structure, order, and hierarchy of a topic | A study of the structure of a democracy |
| Ethics | The issues, debates, bias, and dilemmas related to a topic or discipline | An investigation related to required protective gear in BMX racing |
| Big Ideas | The principles and generalizations of a topic | A study to attempt to define gang activity as an issue of ownership |
| Language of the Disciplines | The specialized terms in the field | A study to investigate the appropriate terms for teeth and dental instruments |
| Relationships Over Time | The connections between the past, present, and future or within a time period | A study of idioms that have developed in language over time |
| Points of View | The awareness of multiple perspectives and opposing viewpoints as ways of seeing and understanding | A study of different points of view related to gun control |
| Interdisciplinary Connections | The relationships between and across disciplines | A study of botany's relationship to ecology |

*Source:* The data in columns 1 and 2 are adapted from *Using the Parallel Curriculum Model in Urban Settings, Grades K–8* (pp. 15–18), by Sandra Kaplan, 2009, Thousand Oaks, CA: Corwin. Copyright 2009 by Corwin. Adapted with permission.

## THE PROCESS OF DIFFERENTIATED INSTRUCTION

Step 1: Examine standards and objectives to be taught. Determine the type of knowledge demanded of the standard and/or objective.

Step 2: Establish the conceptual understanding related to the facts and skills required.

**Step 3: For any fact or skill, determine the level of fluency needed for mastery.**

**Step 4: Design independent student activities that address the facts and skills that are required, along with accommodations for students who need support in achieving mastery of the facts and skills.**

Step 5: Reflect on personal knowledge and attitudes related to resources, the content, and the students.

Step 6: Preassess students in knowledge of facts, skills, conceptual understandings, experiences, attitudes, motivations, and ideas.

Step 7: Determine strategies for instruction at different levels of cognitive processing to include concrete, representational, and abstract processes.

Step 8: Determine the flow of classroom activities to include individual, small-group, and whole-group instruction.

Step 9: Determine benchmarks of student performance, and develop tools for ongoing measurement of progress.

Step 10: Develop selections and criteria for the summative product or performance that accurately reflect the intended outcomes of the unit.

## SUMMARY

Facts and skills make up the foundational level of knowledge and need to be considered differently than conceptual understandings when designing differentiated instruction. Fluency and accuracy are the keys to mastery at this level. Therefore, after initial instruction, the student activities should primarily involve independent practice to master both accuracy and fluency. For some students, however, additional supports and/or instruction are needed. Differentiated instruction may be needed to provide accommodations and strategies to support becoming proficient in the facts and skills. Accommodations and supports at this knowledge level are different from ones provided at other levels of knowledge. In these cases, where accommodations to processing are needed, differentiated instructional focus is on supports that increase fluency of the retrieval of facts and skills rather than true automaticity.

# 4

## *Teacher Self-Assessment*

*To teach is to learn twice.*

—Joseph Joubert, essayist

**B**efore moving into the actual instructional focus, a teacher must also consider a self-assessment in relation to the content and the learners. This assessment can be done before, during, or after the student assessment. It should be done after examining the content and before delivering the instruction. This self-assessment examines personal understandings of the content and levels of mastery. As importantly, it asks about personal attitudes and dispositions regarding both the content and the students.

Ideally, these questions would be a guide for conversations between professionals within the same discipline. The questions lead to rich discussions and shared ideas for approaching instruction. One of the best ways to reflect and increase skills as a professional is through collaboration. It is difficult in some cases to find time to converse professionally; however, collaboration is clearly one of the most valuable actions educators can take. Structuring professional discussions around these questions will increase the depth of conversations and growth as professionals.

The same questions asked here with regard to content can also be used with students to self-assess their understanding of the content before as well as after instruction. The questions can be taken directly the way they are currently presented for students to answer, or they can be changed to voice the perspective of the learner instead of the teacher.

## MULTIPLE APPROACHES TO CONTENT

In order to differentiate instruction, it is necessary for a teacher to have a thorough mastery of the content. The teacher must be able to answer questions and approach the material from multiple levels. In order to help students connect with the material, the teacher must have connections between what is to be taught and other material familiar to the students. A stumbling block with differentiated instruction can occur when the teacher does not have the level of mastery of the content required to differentiate. The teacher only knows one way to teach the material and one perspective of it. This is due to several possible factors. One is the lack of time professionals are given to continuously investigate within their fields. It may be due to a lack of continuing education available for teachers related to the content information. Information is always changing, and it is impossible to keep up with all fields. A teacher is challenged with keeping up with both the most current trends and practices in education along with the most current trends, research, and practices in the field in which he or she teaches. This can often lead to educators relying on the learning experience they have had and simply teach as they have been taught.

Going back to the story involving the process of dividing fractions, a teacher may only be able to teach it by instructing students to take the reciprocal of the second fraction and then multiply the fractions. If the teacher does not possess mastery and true understanding of the division of fractions, there is no way to deliver responsive teaching. When a student asks why the process works, a teacher must be able to explain it in order for students to then understand the concept. When a student needs to have the division of fractions taught in a different way, mastery of the concept is required in order for the teacher to develop alternative learning processes.

The first question to be asked is, "Do I possess a solid conceptual understanding of the material I am teaching?" In order to answer that question, there are some further guiding questions:

- Can I explain the concept to another person?
- Am I confident in being able to answer questions related to the material?
- Can I teach the content through more than one approach?

### Content Connections to Life

The next important consideration is the connection between the content and other concepts. A teacher must be able to guide students to connect the concept being taught to other concepts. This is critical in helping students make the needed connections for real learning to take place. A student needs a place in the brain to store the information, and without the connections to other concepts, there is no ability to develop a schema. Therefore, there is difficulty with mastery, recall, or transference.

In the situation with dividing fractions, when asked, "When is the last time you used the skill of dividing fractions?" there was no one who could correctly connect the process of dividing fractions to any activity. There was the one teacher who said she divides fractions when she cooks; however, it was determined that she actually multiplies fractions in cooking. If the teacher does not have a way to connect to real-life applications, it is unreasonable to think that students learning the material are going to be able to do it.

So, the second question to ask is, "Can I connect the material to other concepts or experiences?" Answering that question would involve answering these additional questions:

- Can I connect this to a real-world application?
- Can I connect this to a concept students have already mastered?
- Can I identify elements of the concept that are the same or different than content the students understand?

## Depth and Clarity of Knowledge

Next, a third question of self-assessment asks about mastery of the content in terms of professional knowledge. This is the most difficult set of questions to ask because "you don't know what you don't know." However, through peer collaboration and discussions or the use of technology to chat with other professionals, there are opportunities to explore these questions. The third question to ask is, "Do I have a clear and accurate understanding in order to teach the concept?"

In an old video made at Harvard University called *A Private Universe* (Sahiner & Filisky, 1987), graduates were asked to explain the phases of the moon or the changes of the seasons. Repeatedly, the answers reflect misunderstandings and inaccurate explanations. The video brings out the fact that we as humans create meaning and explanations for ourselves, and these become powerful factors in our learning. We hold onto beliefs that we have developed even when we have been instructed and provided with a new understanding. The new learning does not necessarily replace past understandings but instead gets assimilated together with the old understandings.

In the teaching profession, it is important to teach accurately so that new concepts are not learned incorrectly. This requires teachers to be vigilant in their discipline and content area. It requires teachers to have mastery at a professional level. Teachers should be researchers using valid sources of information. Before teaching, a teacher must ask this question of accurate mastery. In order to identify any holes or personal misconceptions, this third question must be considered, "Do I have a clear and accurate understanding in order to teach the concept?" Criteria for that would require positively answering the following questions:

- Do I know the most common myths or misconceptions related to the concept?

- Have I researched the concept enough to be able to agree or disagree with secondary sources?
- Do I know my information from valid sources, or have I come to my own conclusions? If I have, do I have research to support my conclusions?
- Do I know the vocabulary and terms used by professionals in the field related to the concept?

## Multiple Perspectives

Finally, a fourth consideration before teaching a concept is that of understanding multiple perspectives related to the content and the students. Without this, differentiated instruction is not possible. A teacher must consider the content from multiple perspectives because a classroom is made up of different perspectives. Each student, because of background experiences and personal explanations, will approach the material differently. As a teacher, the final question to ask related to the concept is, "Am I able to see the concept from multiple perspectives?" The criteria for this would include answering the following questions:

- Do I know the position different groups of professionals take in relation to the concept?
- Do I know the current issues or topics of the professionals in the field related to the concept?
- Can I identify values or cultural beliefs in relation to the concept?

Each of the following four main questions should be asked each time a concept is taught:

- Do I possess a solid conceptual understanding of the material I am teaching?
- Can I connect the material to other concepts or experiences?
- Do I have a clear and accurate understanding in order to teach the concept?
- Am I able to see the concept from multiple perspectives?

It is important to have a clear understanding of the material so that misinformation is not perpetuated. As importantly, in relation to differentiated instruction, without a thorough understanding of the concept, a teacher is limited. There will be less ability to generate materials or use multiple processes to learn or create new connections in learning. Those elements are all aspects to be differentiated in the instructional process.

In reaction to the previous self-assessment questions, a teacher may find the need for research or additional knowledge on a topic. There are resources online that can provide information on current issues and trends on a topic. Before teaching a topic, a quick survey of recently published articles on the topic is a productive starting point. Professional journals also allow teachers to keep up with current research and trends, although their use may be more time consuming. Another great resource is the national professional organization for the particular field. The national organizational Web sites provide information and links to current issues, resources, and experts in the field. For teachers who need more ideas for providing multiple avenues of instruction, peer collaboration through face-to-face meetings or online chats to ask other teachers what works may also be a strong and productive option.

# PERSONAL ATTITUDE OF CONTENT

### Passion

The next area in the self-assessment process is related to personal dispositions regarding the content. Attitude is an important factor in the role of an effective teacher. The feeling a teacher has about content impacts the way the students receive the information. When a person is asked to recall the teacher who had the most significant impact over the course of the person's educational career, and to describe the characteristic that made such a difference, there are three general responses that come up over and over again. One of those three responses is, "The teacher was passionate about what he or she taught." It is important to approach the content in such a way as to find the excitement within the material and communicate that excitement to students. "How do I communicate importance and passion about the content?" Questions related to the value of and passions for the content are simpler and more personal than those about knowledge of content:

- What excites me about the content?
- How can I share my excitement in a way that students recognize? (This may be reflected in the classroom environment and not just in the teaching behaviors.)
- What can I connect within the content to my own life?

### Relevance

Along with that set of questions is the issue of relevance. A teacher must understand the relevance of the topic in relation to oneself as well as the students. When a person is passionate about a content area of study, it is common for that person to see the relevance in his or her own life. For instance, mathematicians tend to see mathematics in everything they do. It is important to question how the content is connected to the students' lives, communities, and cultures. The connections can be either explicitly used in the beginning of a lesson to illustrate relevance, or implicitly, allowing students to create their own personal meaning.

One powerful way to think about this concept of relevance is through storytelling. Many political science and educational researchers are in agreement that, as we look toward leaders of the future, more and more emphasis will be on the skills of storytelling. Leaders of the future will need these intrapersonal skills to captivate audiences and reach people at an emotional level in order to be effective leaders. Therefore, as educators, it will become more and more important to both model these skills as well as help students develop them. Illustrating a concept or lesson with a personal story reflects the relevance of the content in your own life and leads students to make connections to their lives as well. It may be a simple story, but making it real life and true is critical. For example, before teaching a physics lesson, a teacher may tell students about driving to school with a cup of coffee balanced on the console. The teacher explains how he had to slam on the brakes and the laptop and papers fell to the floor while the coffee splashed all over the dashboard. The teacher explains that the lesson for the day will be to discover why the papers and coffee flew forward when the teacher stopped quickly. This brings the concepts to real life. Students can relate to experiences they have had in vehicles that stopped abruptly. The main question is, "How do I see the content in relation to my own experiences and the experiences of the students?" A few additional questions will help you answer this one:

- What experience have I had in relation to the content?
- What experience can I share with students to help them make their own connections?
- What experiences might my students have experienced that are similar to a connection or experience I have had?

## PERSONAL PERSPECTIVES AND ATTITUDES OF STUDENTS

### Knowledge of Students as Learners

The next question is related to the personal understanding of the students. In order to teach effectively, there must be an awareness of the audience. The question is, "What do I know about my students?" This includes more than just the background knowledge of the students and their own understandings of content. The relationships built, as educators and students work through the learning process, cannot be underestimated. It is illuminated through the question asking a person to recall the teacher who had the most significant impact and why. The second of the three most common responses is, "The teacher made me feel special." In order to make students feel special, an educator must take interest in students that goes beyond academic and cognitive performances. This level of knowing the students would also include answering the following questions:

- What setting do my students learn best in?
- What excites my students in their lives?
- What challenges do my students face in their learning?

Knowing the answers to those questions helps develop strategies to motivate and sustain wonder as well as foster learning.

## Expectations

Another aspect to consider is the personal attitude held in regard to the students themselves. This is not in relation to any particular teaching event but is an exercise done as an ongoing monitoring of personal dispositions. These attitudes directly include levels of expectation of the students.

In the widely published Diversity Project at Berkley High School, summarized in *Unfinished Business* (Noguera & Yonemura Wing, 2006), specific hidden inequities were brought to light, including cultural attitude, access to certain courses, and knowledge of the educational system. The project showed that certain students were identified early on as "college material," and teachers talked to those students about getting into college. Other students were never engaged in conversations regarding college applications, course selection, GPA, or scholarships. These conversations were not consistent with actual student performance or achievement. In some cases, students performing very well in school were still excluded from those conversations. The project shows the subtle nature of some inequalities in the educational system. An educator may encourage certain students to try harder courses, call on specific students more often, or provide certain students with special privileges and overlook other students who may also be showing success. Because the behaviors and environmental influences are so subtle, they are easy to dismiss or ignore.

The third and final most-common response when a person is asked to recall the teacher who had the most significant impact over the course of the person's educational career is here. The first was that the teacher was passionate about what he or she taught. The second was that the teacher made the student feel special. The third response most often heard is, "The teacher believed in me and had confidence in my success."

It must be stressed that the following questions are about the expectations of the student rather than his or her ability or performance. The main question to ask every now and then as a self-check is, "Are my expectations for each individual at the height of his or her potential?" Here are other questions to help reflect on this question:

- What do I base my expectations of student performance on?
- Can I separate achievement and potential for learning?

- Do I think of some students as college bound because of their backgrounds and forget other students because of theirs?

These questions are for consideration over a period of time. It is easy to become frustrated with a student's poor performance and ignore it rather than question it. A student who reflects a lack of motivation or seems to have a negative attitude toward learning is even easier to brush aside. Instead, as educators, we need to stop and honor that student with attention to those issues as well. The questions provided here are designed to consider any changes in expectations that have occurred over time for individuals. Variations of these questions can also be used as prompts for student self-reflection over time as well.

Each of the areas in this chapter is important to consider when approaching the planning process. This self-reflection in relation to the content and the students makes a significant difference in the approach to differentiated instruction. Although these questions are designed as a self-assessment, professional collaboration and conversations centered on these questions can prompt new energy and thinking. Talking about each of these questions with a trusted peer can clarify answers to these questions. Professional conversations designed around the content and the students are just as important as the conversations designed around the instruction itself. Involving students in discussions related to these areas also provides insight into the importance of attending to these issues.

# DIFFERENTIATED INSTRUCTION: THE 10-STEP PROCESS

Step 1: Examine standards and objectives to be taught. Determine the type of knowledge demanded of the standard and/or objective.

Step 2: Establish the conceptual understanding related to the facts and skills required.

Step 3: For any fact or skill, determine the level of fluency needed for mastery.

Step 4: Design independent student activities that address the facts and skills that are required, along with accommodations for students who need support in achieving mastery of the facts and skills.

**Step 5: Reflect on personal knowledge and attitudes related to resources, the content, and the students.**

Step 6: Preassess students in knowledge of facts, skills, conceptual understandings, experiences, attitudes, motivations, and ideas.

Step 7: Determine strategies for instruction at different levels of cognitive processing to include concrete, representational, and abstract processes.

Step 8: Determine the flow of classroom activities to include individual, small-group, and whole-group instruction.

Step 9: Determine benchmarks of student performance, and develop tools for ongoing measurement of progress.

Step 10: Develop selections and criteria for the summative product or performance that accurately reflect the intended outcomes of the unit.

## SUMMARY

Self-reflection on professional practices and beliefs is a valuable process and allows a teacher to be more effective. Reflection and conversation, including both the way content is viewed and the way the learners are viewed, help increase effectiveness and responsiveness. There are several aspects to consider related to the content. These include the level of mastery of and passion for the content by the teacher. There are also multiple areas involving the outlooks of teachers with regard to the students. Current, thorough knowledge of content and a passion for teaching the content along with high expectations for students are essential to effective instruction and especially differentiation.

# 5

## Preassessment
## of Students

*The worth of a community, in the long run, is the worth of the individuals composing it.*

—John Stuart Mill

## IMPORTANCE AND
## ROLE OF PREASSESSMENT

Differentiation is a student-based process and a response to students' needs, strengths, knowledge, interests, and learning habits. Without this knowledge of the students, there is no need for differentiated instruction and if instruction were to be differentiated, it would be done randomly and have no basis. Knowledge of the students goes beyond their names and scores on standardized tests. There are several aspects of students that should be considered when approaching differentiated instruction. These aspects should be considered when planning a unit of study and even when teaching a particular concept. The knowledge of students should come from both tools to assess your students as well as observations and discussion. The objective is to obtain information regarding the match between each student and the material to be learned as well as the most effective instructional approach.

In Chapter 2, we discussed facts and skills and the need for the instructor to determine the level of fluency as well as accuracy of the facts and skills. This can be done multiple times and in multiple places throughout the instructional process. A teacher may administer a pretest to determine mastery of facts and skills. Throughout the teaching, these may be checked again. The only time an assessment geared toward instruction would not be fitting is at the end of the instructional process when assessment should focus on mastery. This type of assessment is a summative assessment and reflects what the student has learned. An assessment of conceptual understanding can assess the concepts as well as the facts and skills; however, the focus of the assessment would remain on the concept mastery.

Beyond the curriculum itself, a teacher needs to know what relationship the students have to the content. This includes experiences or background knowledge, the students' learned levels of what they already know, the motivation of the students, the resources the students do and do not have, and any cultural implications to the content. Each of these has a profound impact on the way in which the student interacts and processes the information.

## ASSESSING BACKGROUND CONCEPTUAL KNOWLEDGE

*Background knowledge* is a term used often when talking about the pre-assessment of students. Knowing that past experiences shape how a person knows and views the world, it is important to consider the past experiences of the students in relation to the content. As educators, we may often be surprised about students' understandings or misunderstandings. In the video *A Private Universe* (Sahiner & Filisky, 1987), mentioned in Chapter 4, well-educated students and graduates are asked to explain the concept of the moon's phases or the seasons. The video shows interviewees' vast misconceptions of the concept and introduces a theory about a person's own creation of understanding being more powerful in some cases than any material taught in the classroom. The video shows students, even after being taught the correct information, holding onto their personal inaccurate beliefs and creating a way for the new information to fit the old system of belief. Without uncovering what students currently believe, we can teach excellent lessons, yet they may be stored into improper schema. This creates and reinforces the misunderstandings a person may hold as a truth.

One common strategy for teachers to survey student beliefs is by using a K-W-L (know, want to know, learned) chart. Students write everything they know about a topic on a chart under the letter K. Then, students are asked to generate questions about the topic and record those under the letter W—standing for what the student wants to learn. Finally, after the topic has been taught, the chart is taken out again to add a third column under the letter L—for the information the student has learned.

While a K-W-L chart will activate student thinking about a topic or concept, there are several problems with this strategy. This strategy tries to combine both preassessment and the learning process. Each process is very different and often not compatible in objectives. This process requires students to have correct information before learning new concepts. However, many students write misconceptions and incorrect information about what they know about a topic. By writing and posting these incorrect ideas, the process reinforces the incorrect information. A variation to help somewhat with this issue is to change the letter K to a B, standing for what students believe to be true. This at least opens the door to consider the facts as inaccurate. A second problem with this strategy is that when a concept is being preassessed, it is before instruction has taken place. This strategy requires some understanding of the concept in order to generate questions about it. In many cases, the learner does not know what to ask because there is a lack of knowledge at the start. The student does not know what he or she doesn't know. Therefore, the questions are superficial or contrived for the sake of the process. A final problem with this strategy is that, many times, instructors do not take the time to reflect back on the chart at the end of instruction to record what has been learned. When this process does occur, there is often no connection to the first two columns.

In order to best preassess students, the focus should be on the pre-assessment itself rather than trying to combine it as part of the learning process. Preassessment should drive the instruction. Preassessment and the learning process are two distinct processes that often get blurred, and each becomes less effective. For example, preassessment should always be done on an individual basis to identify where each learner stands. Group work is not appropriate for preassessment, although peer discussions could be appropriate for the purpose of activating thinking about the topic. While cooperative learning does not lend itself well for preassessment purposes, it may be a very appropriate strategy for learning processes.

## CRITERIA FOR PREASSESSMENT

There are defined lines between preassessment and instruction. Figure 5.1 shows the differences between the two processes.

**Figure 5.1**

| Preassessment | Instruction |
|---|---|
| Completed individually | Whole group, small group, and individual |
| Provides a catalyst to recall background knowledge | Applies background knowledge |
| Indicates multiple dimensions of the student's approach to content | Indicates multiple dimensions to student's interaction with content |
| New connections may be made by students but information is not intentionally introduced | Intention is to introduce new information for students to process |

When Jen first started teaching, one of her favorite activities to start a unit with was to have students work in groups to choose a vocabulary word from the upcoming unit and predict the word's meaning. She would then provide an accurate definition and ask students to compare their prediction to her provided definition. She considered this a form of preassessment because she and the students were able to evaluate how close their definitions were to accurate definitions.

After Jen learned more about the purposes of preassessment, she realized she had made some mistakes in considering this a preassessment. While it was a good activity, it was part of the learning process rather than part of the preassessment process. By having students work in groups, she was able to get a general idea of student performance levels but never got any data for individual students. She was not able to use the information from this activity to base instructional decisions on. Jen learned that there were better tools and activities available to her to preassess her students.

Jen changed her activity after this realization. She still used vocabulary words as part of her preassessment. She provided students with the words and related pictures. Students worked independently to match each word with a related picture. The students colored or highlighted the element in the picture to which the vocabulary term was referring. If the student did not know the vocabulary term, they were encouraged to indicate that by leaving the picture uncolored.

The best methods for preassessment involve providing a certain amount of information and asking students what sense they can make of it. One very effective conceptual preassessment is through the use of word-sort activities. Students are provided with a group of words with which they are familiar and are requested to arrange the words into categories or relationships that make sense to the student. The student processes the words and provides a rationale for the groupings. For deeper processing, the process is repeated more than one time. This forces students to think more deeply and more critically about the ideas they have. This provides the teacher with insight regarding the conceptual knowledge the students hold in relation to the concepts to be taught. (See Figure 5.2.)

For students at a primary functioning level who are not reading words, pictures can be used in place of words. For example, if the preassessment involved the types of food on the food pyramid, the pictures could depict types of food. If the preassessment involved animals, animal pictures could be used. Both are examples in which students at all levels have had experiences and will be able to sort the pictures into a variety of categories.

There is no one correct way to complete this type of activity. The purposes are to provide insight into the thinking of the student completing the activity and to assess the current schemas the student has developed in relation to the topic being studied. The words should be familiar ones to the student rather than new terms. This is not presented for the purpose of learning new vocabulary. The criterion for the selection of terms is that the terms be part of essential understandings rather than part of small details related to the topic. There

| Figure 5.2 | Example of a Word Sort for Preassessment of Conceptual Understandings |
|---|---|

Cut apart the following terms and place them into categories. You create your own category title.

| Student | Experiences | Empower | Scaffolding | Standards |
|---|---|---|---|---|
| Resources | Instruction | Concept | Products | Ongoing Assessment |
| Interests | Authentic | Learned Level | Remediation | Skills |
| Enrichment | Relationship | Preassessment | Facts | Adjust |
| Process | Culture | Connections | Motivation | Pacing |

is no set number of words to use. The same process can be done again using vocabulary terms as part of the learning process later in the instructional process. However, the word-sort activity as a preassessment is a good example of when preassessment and instruction should remain distinctly different.

Another related preassessment strategy is to provide a list of conditions and ask students to create predictions. This can be done in any content area. The process of prediction requires tapping into current knowledge, creating new ideas, and making connections between concepts. This provides the instructor with clear direction in teaching. As an instructor, the goal then becomes related to students proving or disproving their own ideas about a concept. Again, this should be used as a preassessment to gain insight into student thoughts, ideas, and beliefs. It should not be used as an instructional activity. (See Figure 5.3.)

| Figure 5.3 | Examples of Predictions as a Conceptual Preassessment |
|---|---|

| Content Area | Situation |
|---|---|
| Science | Here is a glass jar filled with jelly. The air has been vacuumed out. What will happen if I put the jar over a flame for 10 minutes? |
| Social studies | Racial tensions are high. The government has required public schools to desegregate. What might happen in small communities? What might happen in urban communities? |
| Math | Here is a function $X + 2Y$. What would change if Y is a negative number? |
| Literature | The story was written and based in New England in the mid-1800s. What theme will likely be present in this fictional work? |

The strategy of metaphors and similes works in the same way. As a pre-assessment, students can be asked to either create a metaphor or simile about a concept, or the students are provided with one. (See Figure 5.4.) In either case, the rationale for the metaphor or simile chosen is the important aspect that provides information regarding background knowledge. This strategy also provides insight into the levels of understanding regarding a particular concept. Both of these particular preassessment strategies may require accommodations for some students because they rely heavily on verbal skills and possibly written skills. Students may, in fact, know more about a concept than they are able to demonstrate with these strategies due to language and processing limitations. Therefore, these strategies should be used with openness to oral or alternative response modes. Also, it is important to remember that there are no correct or incorrect answers here. This is a preassessment strategy to gain insight into students' thinking processes. It is not appropriate to assign grades or provide correct answers to the prompts.

| Figure 5.4 | Example of a Metaphor or Simile as a Conceptual Preassessment |

| Topic | Simile or Metaphor |
|---|---|
| Differentiated instruction | Differentiated instruction is like football. Explain. |
| Science | Archeologists are like librarians. Explain. |
| Social studies | The Revolutionary War was like David and Goliath. Explain. |
| Math | Music is math and math is music. Explain. |

Using this strategy, students are presented with the simile or metaphor and are simply asked to explain its meaning or provide an interpretation.

## ASSESSING BACKGROUND KNOWLEDGE AT THE FACTS-AND-SKILLS LEVEL

A different approach to preassessment is through the use of a survey-type strategy in which students are simply surveyed in different aspects of a concept. These types of strategies tell more about the facts and experiences a student has with a concept. In selecting a preassessment, there needs to be a determination as to the purpose of the preassessment. It can be to discover any experiences and facts a student has in relation to the concept. It can also be to discover what level of learning the student is at and what the student knows about a topic. There are countless strategies to preassess for facts and skills. These are often more traditional pretest type activities.

## Preassessing Background Knowledge of Facts and Skills

*Form, Function, Facts, and Frills Chart*

Students are asked to complete any boxes in which they are able to provide information given a particular topic. The form section is intended for describing what the topic looks like. The function section is for describing what the topic does or how it functions. The facts area is a place to record specific facts about the topic. The frills box is provided for processing any additional information a student may have on a topic.

| Form | Function |
|------|----------|
| Facts | Frills |

The teacher provides this chart for students to complete with a particular representative topic.

For example, a teacher plans to introduce the skills of using a table of contents. Here is a chart that a student has completed.

### Table of Contents

| Form | Function |
|------|----------|
| • Has chapter names and pages that start each chapter<br>• Has a title | • Tells how the book is organized<br>• Used to find topics in a book |
| **Facts** | **Frills** |
| • It's always in the front of the book<br>• There are different numbers of chapters in tables of contents<br>• It is not specific like the index | • Some books don't have tables of contents<br>• Magazines have something like it but may not call it that |

*ABC Chart*

Given a list of the letters of the alphabet, students write down any associated words they know in relation to a given topic. For instance, a preassessment before a study on the Civil War may look like this:

**A:** Abraham Lincoln, abolish (slavery), amendment (to constitution)

**B:** Battles between north and south

**C:** Civil War, cotton (production), Constitution

**D:** divide, . . .

*Word Underline*

Given a list of words related to a topic, students underline with one line the words they can read and/or have heard of, and they draw a second line under words in which they know the meaning.

For instance, students are going to learn about the skeletal system. They are provided with the following words:

| | | | | |
|---|---|---|---|---|
| femur | cartilage | pelvis | tendon | marrow |
| ligament | radius | patella | calcium | tarsal |

Students draw one line under words they have heard and two lines under words they know.

*Sample Example*

Given a set of words or terms, students provide an example of what the word names. For example, a set of geography terms are listed, and the student writes an example of each term. River: the Mississippi River; Peninsula: Florida, and so on.

*Word Study Block*

Given a particular term, students are asked to provide a definition or picture, characteristics, examples, and nonexamples of that term.

| Definition or picture | Related objects or topics |
|---|---|
| | |
| Opposites | Related patterns or trends |
| | |

For example, students will be studying angles in geometry. A student completes the following that shows accurate understanding of what angles are.

| **Definition:** The figure formed by two rays sharing a common endpoint, called the vertex | **Relationships** |
|---|---|
| | Geometry    Measurement |
| | Architecture    Symmetry |
| | Infinity    Vertex |
| | Lines    Light reflections |
| **Opposites** | **Related Patterns and Trends** |
| | • 90 degrees makes rectangles |
| | • 180 degrees makes perpendicular lines |
| | • 3 angles together that equal 180 can make a triangle |
| | • An angle and its pair equal 360 degrees |

*Technology*

Technology has become a wonderful tool in assisting with all types of assessment. Preassessment tools involving technology are built into many commercial text books. They provide data that can be clearly depicted and easily manipulated. Other technology-related tools besides software are also available and provide practical applications for preassessments. The audience response systems or "clickers" can easily be used to generate answers to prompts quickly and easily from each member of the classroom. Electronic white boards are also unlimited in their ability to provide avenues to allow for student interaction with new material. Each day, technology advances further, and options grow more widely available.

# PREASSESSING MOTIVATION

An often-overlooked area of preassessment is the relevance of a unit of study to students. This becomes tied to motivation and purpose in the learning process. Educators need to consider how the student views the content to be learned. If there is no connection to the student and the content, there is little chance that the student will have mastery of the material to transfer the concept to generalizations. This is both an assessment of the content and the students themselves. Of the content, an educator must ask, "Is this concept one that my students will readily connect with, or is this concept one that will need a lesson to develop those connections?" Of the students, an educator must ask, "Is the student able to see how this relates to his or her self or to experiences in the past or future?"

Related to relevance is the student's motivation to learn something new. There is risk in learning. That is a risk related to failing. There is also risk involved with the social acceptance of learning. That is a risk related to peer pressure and peer status. The first risk is one in which educators can support and respond. The second risk, of peer pressure, allows for less control by the educator, although there are appropriate responses to foster a healthy climate for learning.

Anytime a person tries to learn something new, there is a chance of failure. Many times, there is the experience of failure the first few times. In a nurturing learning situation, the instructor adjusts instruction so that the learner is supported and sees some success for the efforts. A learner must be pushed to the point of challenge that is appropriate and attainable while being challenging to the point of a slight risk. It is the balance of pushing a student to reach—without risking falling flat. It is the balance of challenge without going to the point of frustration. For each student and each task learned, this point is at a different place. It is not only different due to ability but it is also different due to the learner's self-concept and persistence. Each learner is willing to accept a different amount of struggle in learning. Some students never give up, while others stop trying as soon as there is a possibility of not getting something correct. This is both content specific and not just based on personalities. The acceptance of failure can be affected by a number of outside influences. The influences are less important to identify in the preassessment than the degree of willingness to take risks and accept some amount of failure.

The second motivational issue to assess is the social acceptance of learning. In many cases, there is reluctance from students to learn academics due to the lack of social acceptance of being successful in academics. This relationship also needs to be considered when assessing the connection between the learner and the curriculum. While some students have a desire to be recognized for successful academic achievement, there are others who do not want that recognition and will avoid it. This may be due to peer pressure to fit in and not take risks; it may be due to associating academic success with elitism; it may be due to emotional issues or even due to cultural issues. There are countless reasons for a student to not want to appear to perform successfully in academics. No matter the reason, this is an area to consider before designing differentiated instructional approaches.

## STUDENT RESOURCES

Beyond the motivational issues to consider, there are also the personal resources of the student to assess. Students come to school with varying degrees of resources that they are able to tap into in times of need. These resources determine the degree to which a student has or does not have accessibility to personal supports. Each of these resources plays a significant part in student performance and achievement. These resources should also be considered and possibly assessed either formally or informally. The valuable information obtained from an assessment can help assist in instructional decision making for students. Some of these resources include the following:

- Health—Is the student in good health and not suffering from physical pain or hunger?
- Support systems—Does the student have family, friends, or a mentor to access when there is need for positive guidance, encouragement, or decision making?
- Emotional stability—Does the student have strategies and skills to appropriately deal with stress, criticism, failure, acceptance, romance, perseverance, and other situations?
- Economic well-being—Does the student or family have the financial means needed to provide for the necessities of life and academic assignments?
- Cultural understanding—Does the student understand unspoken or unwritten practices and procedures that may be expectations within a culture?

The degree to which a student can access each of these resources will contribute to the likelihood of academic success (Payne, 2005). These are needs all people have in a community, and without these resources, a person faces greater challenges.

In assessing students, each of these resources should also be considered for each student. The degree to which the student does or does not have these resources greatly affects academic performance and motivation to learn. By considering each of these, instruction can be matched to the resources the student has as opposed to adding to student risk and frustration by teaching toward resources not in place. For instance, without financial resources, a student cannot obtain extensive materials for a project. Without emotional stability or strategies, a student will not have the skills to persevere through a long, difficult assignment. Each of these resources affects the learning and teaching process. Therefore, it may be necessary to inventory the resources of a student in order to appropriately differentiate instruction.

## LEARNING HABITS AND PRACTICES

Of course there are plenty of other aspects of both the student and the curriculum that could be assessed in the match between the two. One frequently used avenue of student assessment involves the student's learning style. Being situation specific, a learning style can be difficult to pinpoint when developing differentiated instructional plans. Instead, it may help to identify learning habits, such as

- Focuses on big picture vs. details
- Needs think time vs. needs talk time
- Works best in quiet vs. works best with noise
- Doodles to process vs. takes notes to process
- Needs messy, larger physical space vs. needs neat, organized setting

Students can usually self-identify each one of these. By providing choice on work habits, we teach students not only about differences but also about self-advocacy as well. There are times when each of these characteristics is appropriate in the learning process, and all students should experience each condition. However, there are also times when it matters little to the content but makes a big difference to the learner. Preassessing for this knowledge helps guide instruction through the classroom-management aspect.

As you have seen, when preassessment is referred to as a process within differentiated instruction, it is more than a pretest to identify what a student does and does not know. It is an information-gathering tool used to identify the relationship between the learner and the content as well as instruction. It is an examination of both conceptual and factual knowledge. It examines the student as a learner and the state the student is in when approached with the new material. Knowing this information, about the match between the learner and the content, is essential to differentiating instruction. Without this knowledge, there is no recognized need to differentiate instruction.

We have now added to the process of differentiation, as seen below.

## DIFFERENTIATED INSTRUCTION: THE 10-STEP PROCESS

Step 1: Examine standards and objectives to be taught. Determine the type of knowledge demanded of the standard and/or objective.

Step 2: Establish the conceptual understanding related to the facts and skills required.

Step 3: For any fact or skill, determine the level of fluency needed for mastery.

Step 4: Design independent student activities that address the facts and skills that are required, along with accommodations for students who need support in achieving mastery of the facts and skills.

Step 5: Reflect on personal knowledge and attitudes related to resources, the content, and the students.

**Step 6: Preassess students in knowledge of facts, skills, conceptual understandings, experiences, attitudes, motivations, and ideas.**

Step 7: Determine strategies for instruction at different levels of cognitive processing to include concrete, representational, and abstract processes.

Step 8: Determine the flow of classroom activities to include individual, small-group, and whole-group instruction.

Step 9: Determine benchmarks of student performance, and develop tools for ongoing measurement of progress.

Step 10: Develop selections and criteria for the summative product or performance that accurately reflect the intended outcomes of the unit.

## SUMMARY

Preassessment of students is essential in the process of differentiating instruction. Without knowledge of the students, there is nothing to respond to. Preassessment should include multiple levels and facets. An assessment of base knowledge of the facts and skills along with conceptual knowledge helps design instruction that is responsive to the learners' knowledge levels. Assessments related to their preferences, resources, and experiences allow differentiation to take into account student motivation and opportunities for student success. There are many preassessment activities and strategies that can be used to preassess students without having to rely on traditional pretests.

# 6

## *Instructional Decisions for Differentiation*

*There is a great difference between knowing and understanding; you can know a lot about something and not really understand it.*

—Charles Kettering, inventor

## UNDERSTANDING WHEN AND WHY: NOT JUST SKILLS

The previous chapters spent time addressing the essential processes involved in the planning for differentiating instruction. Without those steps, this chapter simply provides some tools and skills that are elements of good teaching but are not necessarily differentiated instruction. The following story illustrates the rationale and importance for teachers to know why they are developing a particular strategy or best practice for instructing their students.

Two people were observed working at a local town common area. One would work determinedly and dig a good size hole. The other person would follow behind and fill the hole in with as much diligence. They worked up one side of the street, then down the other, working fervently all day. An onlooker was amazed at their hard work but could not understand what they were doing. The onlooker approached the first worker and said, "I am impressed by the effort you two are putting into your work, but I don't get it. Why do you dig a hole only to have your partner follow behind and fill it up again?" The hole digger wiped away some sweat and replied, "I suppose it does look odd. It is because we are normally a three person team, but today the one who puts the trees in the holes called in sick."

Without knowing when or why to select a particular instructional strategy, educators can end up like the two people digging and filling holes—great efforts and practices but little effectiveness. The focus of the professional development is sometimes on the instructional strategies and accommodations, and it frequently fails to provide a focus on when and why to use particular strategies, activities, or tools. Educators are often provided with wonderful instructional strategies and activities along with some direction for effective implementation in the classroom. Teachers are supported with digging holes, planting trees, and filling in holes, rather than on the responsiveness to the conditions in the classroom. As was the case with Jen, her students were completing some wonderful activities; however, Jen was attempting to gather information about her students' learning readiness levels from preassessment and was not able to do so because she had not chosen an appropriate strategy.

## THE LOOK OF DIFFERENTIATED INSTRUCTION

When an administrator asks what differentiated instruction looks like in the classroom, it is difficult to come to any concrete answer. Is it cooperative learning? Is it small-group instruction? Reteaching struggling students? Is it evidence of contracts and independent activities? It could be any one of those and could even be whole-group instruction. The essence of differentiated instruction is not only found in the *what* of happenings in the classroom but also in the *why*. Without addressing the learner and the desired outcome first, there is no rationale for one strategy over another.

Recently, in the age of accountability, there has been a strong emphasis on administrators visiting classrooms for a brief period of time in order to observe snapshots of teaching practices and learning processes. These "walk-throughs" do not allow for a person to truly know if he or she has seen differentiated instruction. A good teaching strategy used without purpose may be completely ineffective. For example, research shows us that cooperative learning can contribute to high learning gains when used correctly. Homework and the use of graphic organizers are other strategies that show promise for higher student learning gains (Marzano, Pickering, & Pollock, 2004). Under that premise, the assumption is that it is great to see a classroom of students participating in cooperative groups, creating graphic organizers, and teachers assigning homework each night. However, if there is no rationale for the student grouping arrangements, if the graphic organizer requires little cognitive processing or is completed by only one group member, or if the homework is something students have not been introduced to, each of those strategies that appears to be so effective through the research is actually ineffective.

Our educational system has been noted for taking hold of a best practice and overusing it or misusing it until it is actually ineffective. An example of this is the whole-language movement that occurred in the early 1980s. What research reflected as good instructional strategies for some learners the educational system pushed for all learners. Teachers were provided with strategies and processes without any rationale or authentic connection to the learning process. Therefore, many educators lost the ability to be responsive to their learners. Ultimately, the strategies proved to be less effective than originally cited due to overuse and misuse.

Just because research shows that bran flakes are healthy does not mean that deep-fried food breaded in bran flakes are healthy—even when the bran flakes are visibly apparent.

## MATCHING THE LEARNER, THE OUTCOMES, AND THE LEARNING STRATEGY AND PROCESS

Rather than focusing on a particular best practice, it is more beneficial to focus on the match between the learner, the type of knowledge to be learned, and the teaching-learning strategy. In order to do this, a solid understanding of the strategies selected along with the intention of the strategy is required. Rather than randomly implementing a teaching strategy for a particular lesson, time and effort should be invested in considering what the desired learning outcome is, what strategy can promote that learning, and how the student can best learn in those situations.

This relationship between the three elements of the student, the desired outcome, and the learning strategy is the platform on which differentiated instruction can occur. The relationship between the learner and the desired outcome provides one stage of differentiation through performance expectation levels. The relationship between the learner and the learning strategy becomes just as important to consider and is a second area in which differentiation can take place. This involves matching the learner to how he or she will learn the facts, skills, or concepts. Finally, the match between the intended outcomes and the learning strategies becomes a third venue for differentiation. In order to reflect on these relationships, it is important to remember that all of them are interdependent, and none are more or less important than the others Figure 6.1 illustrates this interrelationship with the lines between the points being the areas in which differentiation can take place.

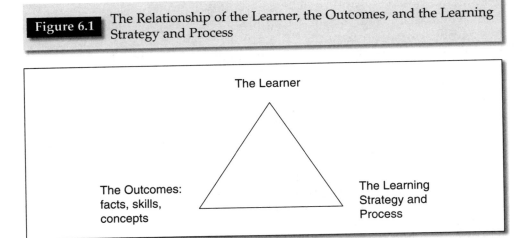

**Figure 6.1** The Relationship of the Learner, the Outcomes, and the Learning Strategy and Process

The Learner

The Outcomes: facts, skills, concepts

The Learning Strategy and Process

The outcomes are defined as the objective or intent of the learning. In most cases, the outcome is mastery of a fact, skill, or concept. The learning strategies are defined as the activities in which the learner participates to acquire new knowledge. The process refers to the learning functions occurring in the brain while the strategies and active learning are taking place.

## LEARNING STRATEGIES AND PROCESSES

Different levels of knowledge require different approaches to teaching and learning. The level of knowledge in which facts and skills are the focus should be approached very differently than conceptual understandings. Facts and skills should be approached using strategies that reinforce, provide practice and repetition, are systematic, and encourage fluency. The end goal for facts and skills involves accuracy and fluency of output. Conceptual understandings must be approached using different methods and strategies. The end goal for conceptual understandings involves the ability to connect and transfer the knowledge to both old and new knowledge. This process, in which students create schema for themselves, demands strategies that allow for cognitive processing to occur. The process focuses on connections within and across both content and context. It allows for the learning of knowledge that can be transferred and applied to multiple situations.

### Processes of Learning

There are distinct learning processes in the brain that work in harmony to create conceptual understandings. Several researchers have established different systems to name intelligences or processes of learning. One of the more simplistic systems to understand is based on three types of processes for learning (see Witzel, 2003). In this system, one recognized learning process is identified as *concrete processing.* This processing involves hands-on learning experiences. It includes learning through tactile and kinesthetic experiences. Tactile processing involves small motor skills, while kinesthetic processing involves gross motor movement. The second distinct learning process is *representational processing.* Representational processing involves learning through graphic and pictorial formats. By processing visual images, the learner makes sense of a concept. The representational processing includes experiences such as using manuals and directions with pictures. It also includes graphics and familiar symbols. A third type of learning process is *abstract processing.* Abstract processing includes learning that depends on language, numbers, or other abstract mediums. Abstract processing requires interpretation and the ability to conceptualize ideas.

Together, these three learning processes work to create complete conceptual understandings. A person may comprehend information through one type of processing but not another, leaving gaps in understanding. For instance, a person may be able to navigate a software program by actually using it but cannot really explain it in words. This person would have successfully processed information at the concrete level but not the abstract level. In another instance, a person may be able to play music but not be able to write it. This person is successful with processing abstractly but not with the representational processing. True mastery occurs when all three forms of processing are successfully accomplished.

Consideration of these processes is important when considering the teaching of conceptual understandings. In order to achieve full mastery at the conceptual level of understanding, all three of these cognitive processes should be proficient. As a teacher, it is important to recognize that there are distinct processes of learning and to identify ways to address each process in instruction. It is also important to consider these processes when implementing ongoing assessment in order to identify which processes are at mastery levels and which are still difficult for the learner.

## Intentional Match of Learning Strategies and Processes

It is not enough to use strategies noted as best practice just because they are good strategies. An instructor must match the strategy with a rationale as to why the strategy is being used. A learning strategy corresponds to a particular process of learning. Instructional thought must first consider the type of learning processing that best meets the needs of a student, and then a particular strategy from within that type of processing should be selected as a structure. There must be a match between the strategy selected and the desired type of thinking process. Figure 6.2 reflects learning and instructional strategies in the processing category along with a statement of intent for each strategy.

| Figure 6.2 | The Processes of Instruction and Their Purposes |

| Concrete Process of Instruction | Purpose of Instructional Strategy |
|---|---|
| Experiments | Develop critical and creative thinking skills |
| Exploration Using Manipulatives | Reinforce knowledge, think about things in a new way, encourage creative thinking |
| Simulation | Develop and foster transference, makes learning personal for increased connections to the content |
| *Representational Process of Instruction* | *Purpose of Instructional Strategy* |
| Graphic Organizers | Process thinking and organize thoughts, personalize learning |
| Visual Representations | Develop executive thinking processes, provide background knowledge, stimulate cognition, reinforce other levels of learning |
| Instructional Modeling | Demonstrate desired outcome, open possibilities for the learner (note: should not be used as a stand-alone strategy) |
| *Abstract Process of Instruction* | *Purpose of Instructional Strategy* |
| Socratic Seminar | Promote divergent and critical thinking and increase skills of seeing multiple perspectives, foster evaluation skills, increase classroom community and acceptance of differences |
| Debate | Promote convergent thinking and increase skills of seeing multiple perspectives, foster prediction skills as well as skills to develop supporting points on a topic, increase team work when done in group settings |
| Concept Attainment | Promote detailed examination, increase critical thinking skills, develop analytical thinking skills |

# LEARNING PROCESSES MATCHED TO OUTCOMES

The concrete, representational, and abstract processing levels provide a systematic way to differentiate instruction as well. The outcome of learning is often either facts, skills, or concepts. Once that outcome has been established, these levels can be considered in adding support or complexity to the learning process. At the fact and skill level, manipulatives, or concrete learning strategies, assist the learner and provide support. These are often seen as accommodations or supports for initial learning. At the fact and skill level, the abstract stages of processing are the most challenging. However, when processing conceptual understandings, it is often the concrete level that is the most challenging. The manipulatives promote student explanations or justifications as to why an abstract concept is true. This act of explaining the rationale or functioning of a concept creates the necessity for higher-level thinking skills. (See Figure 6.3.)

For example, in learning multiplication tables, a struggling learner may be supported in learning by using manipulatives to reflect groups of numbers and to provide a visual for counting. The objects support the learner in the acquisition of the facts and skills. When learning the concept of multiplication, however, a student may be able to readily calculate multiplication facts at an abstract level but can be challenged to create a model of how multiplication works in the patterned system of numbers.

Therefore, differentiation can take place in several formats. The processing can be differentiated for different learners. Some may be at a concrete stage while others are at a representational stage and still others at an abstract stage. Responsiveness would include different sets of activities or learning processes for each of those groups. Beyond that, there are also students at different levels of complexity within the same learning process. Some students may be struggling with a concept and must rely on the representational stage while others need greater challenge and work with the concrete learning process. There could even be students struggling with learning and in need of concrete manipulatives for support while others in need of additional challenge could also use concrete manipulatives to extend conceptual understandings.

| **Figure 6.3** | The Functions of Three Learning Processes for Facts, Skills, and Concepts | | |
|---|---|---|---|
| | *Concrete* | *Representational* | *Abstract* |
| **Facts and Skills** | For learning and support—provides accommodations | To connect the concrete to the abstract | For the solving of problems |
| **Concepts** | To manipulate and explore a concept—challenge students to explain and justify procedures and solutions | To organize thought processes through personal design and to communicate ideas | To analyze and make connections within and outside of the concept |

The template on page 68 (Figure 6.4) provides a framework for the process of planning for different learning processes for different learners. This template is not necessarily meant for daily planning. Its purpose is to frame the thinking about planning the learning activities and strategies for differentiated instruction.

**Figure 6.4**  Framing Template for Strategic Decision Making

| Standard/objective: | |
|---|---|
| **Big idea:** | |
| **Facts or skills:** | **Concepts:** |
| **Level of fluency needed for mastery:**<br><br>☐ Automatic<br>☐ With think time<br>☐ With cues<br><br>**Notes:** | **Background knowledge and other skills required:** |
| **Strategies for practice and support:**<br>(Frequently independent student work)<br><br>*Strategies for teaching facts and skills along with the use of accommodations are included in Chapter 2* | **Strategies for instruction:** |
| | **Concrete processing:** |
| | Desired outcome:      Strategy: |
| | **Representational processing:** |
| | Desired outcome:      Strategy: |
| | **Abstract processing:** |
| | Desired outcome:      Strategy: |

*Note*: A reproducible version of this form appears on page 135 of the Appendix.

Let's take a look at our teacher, Jen, and her thoughts as she works through this process and completes this chart. As teachers practice these metacognitive processes and become familiar with the questions to be asking, the process becomes more natural and takes less time. Working in collaboration with another professional also makes the process more effective and less demanding for a teacher.

---

## Example of the Metacognitive Process of a Teacher

Jen begins the process by looking at the state and local standards she is required to address during the semester. She is teaching physical science and must teach her students about states of matter. She reads the standard that says, "Students will identify four states of matter and recognize that changes in state can occur." Jen understands the simplistic nature of this standard. She realizes that these are just a set of facts and she needs to increase the level of knowledge in order to provide a quality learning experience. She asks herself why it is important for students to know this, and she determines that the real idea here is about states of matter being able to change when conditions change. She asks herself again why that is important for her students to learn and how it could apply to their lives. She thinks that she can take a different approach or lens for this standard and teach her students the idea that outside factors influence and can create powerful change. She is satisfied with this and sees how that could connect to events in history, characterization in literature, mathematical functions, team sports in PE, and music history. She is satisfied that now she has something to work with.

Her next step is to determine the facts and skills required for that standard. She comes up with this list:

- There are four states of matter: solid, liquid, gas, and plasma.
- Temperature plays a role in determining states of matter.
- Combining matter can affect the state.
- Data collection is needed to document change.

She thinks about her students and what they may or may not know in relation to these facts. She thinks some of her students may know a few, and others will have no exposure to these. In order to find out what they know, she will need to do a preassessment. She determines that she will have students create a table that reflects predictions of change in states of matter when certain factors are provided. She comes up with the following preassessment that students will complete on their own so that she can assess their level of knowledge of the related facts:

| Matter | Influence | Prediction: What will happen? |
|---|---|---|
| Solid | Heat is added | |
| Liquid | It is stirred vigorously with a machine for 10 days | |
| Gas | It is trapped, and pressure is added | |
| Plasma | Oxygen is removed | |
| Liquid | Combine with a solid | |
| Provide an example you know for each of the following: | | |
| Solid:<br>Liquid:<br>Gas:<br>Plasma: | | |

As she creates this preassessment, she also thinks about the level of fluency needed for mastery of the facts. She determines that students must be able to quickly name the states of matter. She also wants them to be able to generate an example of each state of matter when asked within 10 seconds. She decides that determining the results in changes in matter do not have to be fluent, but accuracy is important.

Before having students complete this on their own, she wants to build some background knowledge to trigger any ideas students have about states of matter. Therefore, she thinks about how these facts relate to her students and what experiences the students may have had that could relate to the topic. She determines that before she presents the preassessment she will provide the following riddle:

On June 15, woman claimed she had her car broken into, but the police thought she was not telling the truth. They questioned the woman, who said, "I went to the store where I go each week to get chocolate I get for my mother. I took it out of the bag and put it on the dashboard of my car so that I would not forget to bring it to her after work. When I came out of my office after work, I saw a person running from my car and there was a piece of wrapper on the ground next to the car." The police could not find the wrapper, or any sign that the car had been broken into. However there was no sign of the chocolate either. After listening to her story in the afternoon heat, the police became frustrated and were more suspicious of the woman than before. What was wrong with her story?

Students should be able to conclude, with some guiding questions and detective work, that putting a chocolate bar on the dashboard of a car in June would likely melt the chocolate. While students are being introduced to the concepts with her riddle, Jen will use appropriate terms and explanations, although at this point she will provide little instruction directly related to the desired outcomes.

During this planning stage, Jen also thinks about her own knowledge of states of matter. She realizes she is not sure what the criterion is to determine plasma from a gas or solid. She needs to research this before teaching. She also thinks about other ways she can teach this besides just using forms of water and temperature changes. She makes a note to ask the veteran teacher next door how she has taught this effectively in the past.

Knowing that this is just the fact and skill aspect of her teaching, Jen thinks about strategies students will implement to reach mastery of these facts. She determines that two experiences with changing matter done as experiments will be enough to address these facts. This learning will take place as a simple observation of cause and effect. Jen recognizes that students will require practice in order to master the skills. Therefore, she will also set up some independent centers and a take home project to practice and reinforce these facts. The centers will include students watching videos on the topic of states of matter and designing a cartoon strip that involves an incident as a result in changes of matter. Students will also have practice and reinforcement of these facts by completing an experiment with gelatin in their kitchens at home with their families.

Moving back to the conceptual understanding, while students are working to master the facts of changes in states of matter, Jen's instructional focus will be on the concept and big idea she identified earlier. This is that matter can change when conditions change. Her big idea was, "Outside factors influence and create powerful change." This concept requires different teaching strategies than the strategies used for mastery of facts and skills. Jen thinks about the strategies used specifically to develop conceptual understandings. She also reflects on the information she knows about different learning processes in the brain before selecting her instructional approach for conceptual mastery.

When Jen develops her lesson at the conceptual level, she seeks a way to address the concept that matter can change when conditions change. She asks herself, "How can this concept be experienced by students in the three processes of concrete, representational, and abstract?" Before deciding on instructional strategies to provide experiences at all three conceptual levels, Jen also needs to think about what skills she wants her students to develop through the learning process. She understands that her instructional strategy is twofold: (1) to provide a venue for conceptual learning of content to take place and (2) to develop lifelong learning skills and cognitive processes. Therefore, Jen considers her students and the strategies before making the instructional decisions.

After these considerations, Jen decides that the concrete level will include some hands-on explorations with a gooey substance. Students can introduce different conditions to the substance and predict the outcomes. At the representational level, students will need to process the information through graphic formats. At this level, students will create graphic organizers showing initial condition of matter by drawing a pictorial representation, indicating the condition introduced, and then draw the new condition of the same matter. At the abstract level, students will use words and language to connect this learning to other disciplines through the use of a state-catalyst-result booklet. This booklet will be a flipbook cut into three sections with a term or word on the first section, a catalyst that is introduced in the second section, and the result in the third section. Students can complete this with references to literature, science, history, personal experience, or any other ideas that reinforce the concept.

The focus of these activities is both to gain a conceptual understanding and develop specific cognitive skills. While each of these learning activities requires teacher direction and structure, the responsibility for learning is placed directly on the student. The student is interacting with the cognitive processes, and, therefore, the ownership is on the part of the student and not the instructor.

Figure 6.5 is Jen's completed template of her process:

**Figure 6.5**   Completed Framing Template for Strategic Decision Making

| | |
|---|---|
| **Standard/objective:** Students will identify four states of matter and recognize that changes in state can occur. | |
| **Big idea:** Outside factors influence and can create powerful change. | |
| **Facts or skills:**<br><br>• There are four states of matter—solid, liquid, gas, and plasma.<br>• Temperature plays a role in determining states of matter.<br>• Combining matter can affect the state.<br>• Data collection is needed to document change. | **Concepts:**<br><br>Matter can change when conditions change. |
| **Level of fluency needed for mastery:**<br><br>☒ Automatic<br>☐ With think time<br>☐ With cues<br><br>**Notes:**<br><br>Also need to be able to generate examples in 10 seconds | **Background knowledge and other skills required:**<br><br>• Activated with riddle about chocolate bar left in the car<br>• Must know sources of heat, definition of matter |
| **Strategies for practice and support:**<br><br>(Frequently independent student work) | **Strategies for instruction:**<br><br>**Concrete processing:**<br>Hands-on play with gooey substance |

| | |
|---|---|
| • Two in-class activities in which students observe cause and effect<br>• Center with videos on states of matter<br>• Center creating cartoon strip on state of matter changing<br>• Lab at home using gelatin | **Desired outcome:** Experience changes of matter    **Strategy:** Exploration Explore and predict |
| | **Representational processing:** |
| | **Desired outcome:** Indicate direct cause-effect relationships    **Strategy:** Graphic organizers for cause and effect of matter |
| | **Abstract processing:** |
| | **Desired outcome:** Transfer learning to other disciplines    **Strategy:** Concept attainment Creation of a flip-book |

Good teaching is more than implementing best practices and delivering content. Powerful instruction is planned and deliberate. It takes into consideration the multiple facets within the relationships of the learner, the learning processes, and intended outcomes. Differentiation practices match those relationships systematically and deliberately designed to meet the needs of individual students working toward a desired outcome. Teaching, like gourmet cooking, is the art of taking a desired outcome, combining multiple ingredients, and considering the interactions of those ingredients to create a masterful product. The process itself determines the quality of the product.

# DIFFERENTIATED INSTRUCTION: THE 10-STEP PROCESS

Step 1: Examine standards and objectives to be taught. Determine the type of knowledge demanded of the standard and/or objective.

Step 2: Establish the conceptual understanding related to the facts and skills required.

Step 3: For any fact or skill, determine the level of fluency needed for mastery.

Step 4: Design independent student activities that address the facts and skills that are required, along with accommodations for students who need support in achieving mastery of the facts and skills.

Step 5: Reflect on personal knowledge and attitudes related to resources, the content, and the students.

Step 6: Preassess students in knowledge of facts, skills, conceptual understandings, experiences, attitudes, motivations, and ideas.

**Step 7: Determine strategies for instruction at different levels of cognitive processing to include concrete, representational, and abstract processes.**

Step 8: Determine the flow of classroom activities to include individual, small-group, and whole-group instruction.

Step 9: Determine benchmarks of student performance, and develop tools for ongoing measurement of progress.

Step 10: Develop selections and criteria for the summative product or performance that accurately reflect the intended outcomes of the unit.

## SUMMARY

The process of designing differentiated instruction includes determining specific strategies for instruction rather than teaching with strategies that are random or not based on research. Differentiated instruction requires that the instructional strategy used matches the learner and the intended outcome of the teaching. Different strategies provide for different opportunities and learning experiences to take place. The selection of the instructional strategy is as important as the selection of the content and materials used. This is the most frequently overlooked aspect of instruction, and yet it is critical to successful learning. Intentionality must be exercised when selecting strategies and methods for teaching and the student learning process.

# 7

## *Management of Flow*

*He who would learn to fly one day must first learn to stand and walk and run and climb and dance; one cannot fly into flying.*

—Friedrich Nietzsche

Possibly the most neglected aspect of differentiated instruction in professional development is classroom management. The understanding of how to address many different needs at the same time while maintaining control of the classroom may seem to be a daunting task. It may also be the most critical aspect toward the contribution of a successful experience for both the teacher and the students. Classroom management includes the choreography of the flow within the class. It involves the transitioning between whole-group instruction, small-group instruction and individualized instruction. Being able to manage that flow and knowing when to transition are deliberate and planned teaching acts that require preparation and knowledge of the content as well as the students.

Within whole-group and small-group instruction, there are different levels of support that can be provided. The supports will vary in duration and intensity. One way to look at these levels of support is through a model of the gradual release of responsibility. In many instances, some whole-group teaching is required by the teacher. This is most important when a new concept, fact, or skill is being introduced. Students may need to have the new learning taught explicitly and modeled before experiencing it and attempting it on their own. The students then transition to taking on the active learning with the teacher supporting or coaching the student. This model supports effective instruction through a transfer from the teacher being responsible and active to the students taking on the responsibility for their learning. This transition is done over the course of the learning process. This model can be considered when differentiating instruction because it provides a systematic framework in which to support learners while they strive for independence. In some cases, the time in which learning is passed over to student responsibility is short, and in other cases there are supports needed for extended time and throughout the transition. The stages of the gradual release of responsibility can be seen in Figure 7.1.

**Figure 7.1**    The Gradual Release of Responsibility

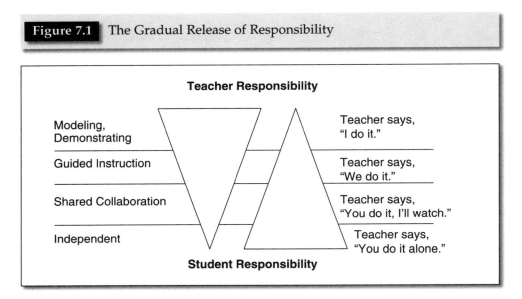

## WHOLE-GROUP INSTRUCTION

Whole-group instruction often has a stigma attached to it because it is often used synonymously with *lecture.* Many educators are concerned about the overuse of whole-group instruction; and in some cases, administrators frown on this choice of instructional delivery. Research tells us that students learn best by experiencing and "doing." Students can be activity involved even within whole-group instruction. Using this model of gradual release of responsibility, it becomes apparent that whole-group instruction can occur at any stage of the release of responsibility process as well. Whole-group instruction has an important and valid place in our classrooms. Awareness of the purpose and timing are essential in justifying this instructional delivery model.

Whole-group instruction should be used when the instruction needs to be consistent for all learners. Giving directions, for instance, is a time when whole-group instruction is effective and efficient. In planning a lesson, whole-group instruction should be considered as an instructional delivery model before or after a time when students have been engaged in independent practice of the facts and skills needed for a lesson or before or after small-group instruction. Whole-group instruction may not last for an entire class period and should be designed with the intent of actively engaging students. It should be focused on directions, explanations, or direct, explicit instruction.

Many times the teaching strategy selected for whole-group instruction is lecture. The amount of time spent using lecture as a strategy for instruction depends on the students' attention spans and the intensity of the processing of new information. This model of gradual release of responsibility reinforces the need to move beyond the modeling and demonstrating tier so that students become responsible in the learning process. At the second tier of this model, the learning process begins to transfer, and the responsibility is shared. Whole-group instruction may also be implemented through guided instruction.

Whole-group instruction is not simply limited to the lecture teaching strategy or the modeling level of instruction. Whole-group instruction also includes instruction in which students are active participants. In the diagram in Figure 7.1, it may be part of the shared learning tier as well. One example of whole-group instruction at the shared collaboration level of support is through the use of response cards or electronic response systems. Using these, the teacher is still instructing the whole group; however, each student responds and interacts with the content through the use of the card or keypad. All three levels of support may be provided through whole-group instruction.

### Example of the First Part of a Daily Lesson Schedule Using Whole Group Instruction

9:00–9:10: Students get settled in seats and complete independent practice work.

9:10–9:20: Whole-group instruction and new instruction presented through lecture and modeling. **(modeling/demonstrating)**

9:20–9:25: Teacher walks students through the process while students follow along completing the process at their seats, while continuing with whole-group instruction. **(guided instruction)**

9:25–9:40: Students try the process on their own with the watchful eye of the teacher, who circulates to observe students. **(shared collaboration)**

## DIFFERENTIATION IN WHOLE-GROUP INSTRUCTION

Using the stages of gradual release of responsibility and accommodation strategies, differentiated instruction and whole-group instruction are not contradictory. While guided instruction is taking place for some students, others can be given the freedom to work independently or with minimal monitoring. While the instruction is at the stage of shared collaboration, the teacher may provide guided instruction or modeling for some struggling students as they are observed in their work. The goal is for the students to work at the independent level as soon as they are able to. If the student falters, the framework is in place to move back to a level of more intensive support.

Providing accommodations is another way to differentiate within whole-group instruction. Generally, accommodations during whole-group instruction are implemented in the form of adjustments to the environment or in the presentation of the learning objectives by the instructor. These changes are made based on individual student needs in order to help a student experience success. Oftentimes, a teacher discovers that an accommodation made in the presentation to help one student will help several or all students simultaneously. Sometimes, the teacher then makes the accommodation part of his or her regular presentation style. For instance, a science teacher began providing a partially completed outline for a student who struggled to write notes during her lectures. She soon realized that this would benefit all the students, so she began providing the partial outlines for all students in the class. What she found was that the students could focus more on the scientific concepts than on the note taking. What started as an accommodation for one student became a routine instructional strategy and successful practice, which many students found beneficial.

Accommodations related to whole-group presentation include but are not limited to

1. Providing a cloze passage or partially completed outline for note taking;

2. Explicitly using a strategy for organizing notes, vocabulary, and questions such as Cornell note taking;

3. Writing key terms, phrases, and page numbers for a visual cue rather than depending only on oral presentation;

4. Providing a graphic representation;

5. Anchoring ideas in space through physical and positional gestures;

6. Explicitly using think-aloud strategies to provide metacognitive guidance;

7. Highlighting important ideas verbally using a verbal cue such as, "This is a very important statement";

8. Recording the oral presentation for students to access for play back later;

9. Reinforcing the presentation with the use of video, visualizations, artifacts, or technology; and

10. Moving while presenting to use proximity to emphasize important points.

While these accommodations are necessary for some learners to experience success, they may not be needed by other students. Those students who need the accommodation will take advantage of it and must be encouraged to make use of such support. Those who do not need the accommodation will often not even notice it. In each of these cases, a student needing the accommodation will benefit, and the student who does not need it will not be held back in any way.

Accommodations to the environment can be more difficult to implement. While accommodations are based on what each student needs for supports to be successful, the needs of different students in the class can be contradictory. One student may need the room very quiet while another may need white noise. Accommodations related to the student's place for learning can also be difficult. There are only so many front row seats!

However, there are adjustments that can be made to the learning environment during whole-group instruction that may support some learners.

---

Accommodations to the environment include but are not limited to

1. Providing seating in a spot with fewer distractions or less traffic;

2. Allowing tactile learners to hold "fidget toys" while listening;

3. Allowing students to doodle while listening;

4. Providing comfortable seating either with alternatives to desk chairs or by providing cushions for the chairs;

5. Allowing for input on preferred lighting when possible to control;

6. Hanging consistent visual cues on the walls in an organized, resourceful system so students can use the cues as a resource and know where to look for a cue;

7. Creating an environment that celebrates questions and expects mistakes; and

8. Providing opportunities for discrete responses, such as response cards or electronic response systems.

---

## SMALL-GROUP INSTRUCTION

After any whole-group instruction is completed, it is best to follow it with practice, reinforcement, or a student-centered activity related to the direct instruction. Students benefit when they are able to interact with the material presented in a whole-group setting. In the model of the gradual release of responsibility, student participation includes guided instruction, shared collaboration, and independent practice. These levels of support transition the responsibility from the teacher to the student. It is not expected that all students are readily able to make the leap from observing a model or demonstration to independent practice. The rate at which students move through these levels of support and the amount of support provided for each student is different for each student and each learning experience. Therefore, differentiation is needed to adjust the levels of support, the pace, and the intensity of the support.

By observing students as they move through these levels of support, a teacher can identify areas of strengths and needs as well as determine the amount of support each learner needs in order to experience success in the lesson outcomes. Through observation and data collection, similarities in learners' performances, needs, interests, or habits of learning can be collected. These similarities will become the basis for the creation of small groups.

One of the common myths in the area of differentiated instruction is that it is synonymous with small-group instruction. While small-group instruction is a component of differentiated instruction, differentiated instruction is more than just working in small groups. Further, small-group instruction for the sake of group work is not necessarily differentiated instruction at all. In order for small-group instruction to be aligned to differentiated instruction, there must be a rationale for the formation of the small groups.

There are several effective practices of cooperative grouping in the field of education. However, grouping by chance, coincidence, or a commonly used practice of grouping a high student, a low student, and two average students together is not differentiated instruction. The purpose of those groups is for community building rather than instruction. Such models can also provide some excellent classroom management strategies. Classroom management and community building both have very important roles in a classroom and should not be ignored. However, group work of that nature should not be confused with small-group, differentiated instruction.

Small-group instruction provides many opportunities to provide differentiation. Groups can be based on a number of attributes. Groups can take the form of classroom centers or cooperative activities. They can also be groups designed so that a particular group of students receives specific instruction.

## INDIVIDUAL INSTRUCTION

Besides thinking that all small-group instruction is differentiated instruction, there is a strong myth related to individual instruction. When some people hear the term *differentiated instruction*, they may think that the instruction is different for each student. This misconception leads some to believe that a good teacher who differentiates instruction does different

Following are some of the areas to consider for creating differentiated groups:

1. The abilities of different students on a particular task—some may need enrichment, and others may need remediation or reteaching;

2. The background experiences students may or may not have that are necessary for learning a particular concept;

3. The language of students;

4. The rate at which the students learn;

5. The preferred work environment—some like to talk through ideas to learn and others want processing time;

6. The learning modalities preferred for learning a particular task—visual, tactile, kinesthetic, the eight multiple intelligences, and so on;

7. The interests and motivators of different students; and

8. The preferred media in which to obtain information—Internet, video, text, and so on.

lesson plans for each student. That is certainly not the case. Differentiated instruction involves like instruction with students experiencing learning in different ways. The key to individual instruction is in providing choice or options within a designed structure or framework.

There are several ways in which a teacher can control the learning outcomes and still provide student choice. Examples include contracts or interest-based projects.

## Contracts

Generally contracts provide a menu of options for a student. Each student is able to pick from the "menu." However, there are guidelines set to determine the parameters for the choices. Students may be required to select different options from different categories or select a specific total number of items or point values. It is important that these guidelines are made clear to the students. On page 82 is an example of a student contract for a middle school language arts class.

## Literature Contract

After completing your required reading, select any four of the following:

1. Create a Venn diagram comparing your main character to the leadership traits you have been examining in our biography study.

2. Develop a graphic representation of the main elements of setting that influence the story. Use labels to clarify the most critical elements.

3. Create a T-chart to indicate the outcomes of the story as written and the outcomes if the story had taken place in the Baroque era.

4. Write a paragraph to explain your reaction to the story as it built. Describe your abilities to relate to characters, predict outcomes, and react to the storyline.

5. Compare and contrast the nature of conflict in this story to the nature of conflict in another story you have read. You may present this in any way you choose.

6. In any format that makes use of technology, create a product for the main character giving advice to him or her.

7. Create eight important questions that could be used as a book study for the book you read.

8. Create a review of your book with your peers as the audience. The review must give a description of the story line, main character, conflicts, and your opinion of the book. It cannot give away the ending of the book.

The four products will be due on Thursday, February 24.

Cut here and turn in when you have committed to your four choices.

Name: _____

I have selected to do the following four projects by number: _____

I will have these done by the due date. If I encounter obstacles that I cannot resolve on my own, I will come to you before the date that these are due.

Signed, _____

# INTEREST-BASED PROJECTS

With carefully identified objectives, students are able to develop a project based on their own interest that meets specific learning objectives. For instance, if the learning objective involves identifying characteristics of prominent leaders, students may choose a leader of their choice to identify those traits. If the learning objective involves recognizing traits of nonfiction text, students can pick a nonfiction text of interest in order to recognize the commonalities. In implementing these types of choices, it is imperative that the learning objectives are clear in order to avoid random learning activities with no intended direction. Once the objectives are clear, different materials based on student interest can be used.

It is time to take a look at Jen again. Let us conclude this chapter with a visit to Jen's class and see how she responds to her learners and the objectives using the three modes of differentiated instruction.

---

## Meet Jen's Class

At last, it is finally time to meet Jen's students and see her in action. She has planned well-designed lessons and thought about her student's strengths and needs. Now, she is ready to implement instructional practices. This is where "the rubber meets the road." Jen will move back and forth between whole-group, small-group, and individual instruction in order to meet the needs of her students and manage the learning activities in her classroom. Welcome Jen's students . . .

The first student to enter the room is Ben, who races everyone into the building. He breaks the school rules and runs down the hallway with his backpack half open, oblivious to the papers falling out in all directions along the way. He noisily enters the classroom and announces that he is the first one in the room for the 10th straight day. Once he enters, he begins wandering around the room as if it is the first time he has been here and touches anything and everything that catches his eye. He drops his backpack on the floor, although he knows very well where it should be stowed since he has been reminded of the routine for the past eight weeks of school. Ben takes medication at home each morning related to his hyperactivity.

Ben is followed by a group of four boys, Jon, Elijah, AJ, and Tim. These four boys play baseball together. Jon and Tim have backpacks and are well dressed. They are both average performing students in their academics. Elijah and AJ arrive with no backpacks, and AJ has noticeably worn clothes. AJ is two years older and much larger than his peers, having been retained twice. He does not like school and is unmotivated to do most pencil-and-paper activities. Elijah struggles with reading and reads more than two years below grade level. He also does not enjoy most academic work, and both he and AJ have recently been receiving more intensive interventions by a reading specialist at the beginning of each day.

Next are the social butterflies—a group of three girls who are inseparable. Melissa and Shauna have been in the same class for the past three years, and the third, Brianna, just moved to the school and has attended more than seven schools to date. She is older and more mature than the other two but also more insecure despite the fact that she has earned nothing other than As through her school career. Academics come easily to her.

Behind the three girls are two, Maria and Lillie, who speak Spanish as their native language and have no adult family members who speak English. Maria often translates for Lillie because Lillie is more limited in her English, having moved from South America within the past six months. Lillie receives additional services weekly from the English language specialist.

Next is Aidan, who walks in slowly with his nose buried in a book. He is identified as gifted and works in all academic areas well above grade level. One day a week, Aidan attends a gifted program with other students identified as gifted. Behind Aidan is Emily with her mom. The mom explains that she came in to be sure that Emily would be getting her work for the next week so that she could take it on the family cruise vacation they are taking. Emily is a good student and has high potential but is often distracted by other events such as vacations, dance, music classes, girl scouts, horseback riding, cheerleading, and soccer.

Finally, in the back of the pack is Julia, who is on crutches after breaking her ankle while skating. She is being helped by her three closest friends, Kaylee, Scott, and Bo. Scott is usually the last to come in due to his physical handicaps. He has braces on his legs as a result of a birth defect. He also receives speech/language therapy for oral communication and articulation and is difficult to understand without the use of gestures. Kaylee also has an IEP and has been identified as having a learning disability, making many academic experiences a struggle for her. Bo is the class clown and entertains his peers but is often in trouble for inappropriate behavior. He has his own behavioral plan in place with a reward system.

After all the students arrive and finish their morning routines to get settled, Jen wants to grab their attention right away to pique their interest in a new unit she is planning to begin. Her unit is a study of civilizations, and one of the conceptual understandings she wants students to master is a correlation between the tools of a civilization and the needs and values of the civilization. Jen tells her students that they will be able to each get their own cell phone if they can come up with a way to convince the communications store that they need these phones. She divides her students into groups in order to create charts of as many reasons why they need cell phones as they can generate.

She creates one group with Brianna and Aidan, who are both higher performing students, and adds AJ, who is also older and who is really wanting a cell phone. She rounds out this group with Bo because he looks up to AJ and will be more likely to stay on a task if AJ is also engaged in it.

She also creates a group made up of Lillie, Kaylee, Emily, and Shauna. Her reason for creating this group is to provide additional support by working with them to guide their thinking. She knows Lillie, who is just learning English, will need supports with the vocabulary. Kaylee and Emily will both benefit from more explicit and direct teaching as Kaylee struggles with inductive reasoning, and Emily needs to get the point of the unit before leaving on her trip. Shauna is there to ensure that she works with other students besides her best friend Melissa. As a teacher, Jen will help guide discussion through questioning techniques and providing different suggested perspectives to consider.

The other two groups of four students are based more on social factors and behavioral issues. Each group has a natural peer leader, and peer supports will be a primary method to get the task complete.

The students complete this group task and share out with the other groups using a strategy called *carousel*. Each group leaves their chart at their worktable. On signal, the groups move in a clockwise direction and stop at the next worktable. They read the product of the group who left their work, and they write any comments on notepads to leave with the chart. On the signal, groups rotate again to the next station, read the chart along with the other group's comments, and add to those comments. Students move as a group when a signal is given until they have had a chance to review all charts and comments.

Jen then begins her whole-group discussion about the ideas generated. She provides a guided lecture with key terms posted. She leads students to realize that the needs that they came up with are the same ones that, for the most part, originally triggered the invention of the cell phone. She guides them to draw the conclusion that the needs and wants of the people drive invention. She then shows them a short video segment from the Internet on this concept.

While Jen is organizing her materials for students to begin independent work, she asks them to respond in their journals using either sentences or a graphic organizer to explain how the cell phone activity can be related to ancient civilizations' need for the cutting tool developed in ancient time. She will review these journals after school to see how well students are grasping the concept. Tomorrow, she will group students according to the depth of their response. For those who did not understand, she will begin the day reteaching them. Those who understand the connections will be grouped to discuss and record thoughts on other current-day inventions that have developed from a need.

For today, however, the lesson continues with independent work. Jen wants these new ideas reinforced and developed. She provides three assignments for students. Brianna, Aidan, and Emily are each going to randomly select a human need that has been written on a piece of paper and put in a cup. For instance, one reads, "need for more accurate communication." These students will generate a timeline of progress indicating as many inventions over time that they can think of that have been developed from that need. On another day, the products they generate will be the basis for a closer examination of civilizations over time in relation to those inventions. Emily, who will be leaving for vacation, is included in this group so that she can use this product for her upcoming assignment while she is away.

Jen provides a second task for her more struggling learners. This group of students will each be given a limited choice of inventions from which to choose, and each will create a list of all the needs that the invention may serve. For example, one paper says, "ballpoint pen," and the student creates all the needs met by a ballpoint pen. Although Maria, who speaks Spanish more than English, is not considered a struggling learner, she is in this group because Jen wants to be able to provide her with vocabulary support needed to define and describe inventions that may be from hundreds of years ago.

Jen's third activity will be for students mainly on grade level. These students will be creating a graphic organizer suited to chain events. They will each be given a different invention and will create a chain of cause and effect, creating a line of need-invention-need-invention for at least four links. For instance, if given the invention of a telephone, the need before it could be listed as a need to communicate verbally over long distances. Then, the invention of the phone caused people to want to move around their homes more than the cord would allow. This in turn, sparked the invention of the cordless phone. Students would be encouraged to create their own graphic organizer, but there would be a standard one provided as well. As an accommodation, Ben, who is easily distracted, would be encouraged to use symbols and abbreviations to get his thoughts on paper and stay on task. He as well as others would be able to access detailed pictures of their invention using computers or actually hold the invention if available.

While students are working, Jen provides a set of guiding questions for all students in the event that a student gets stuck. She also facilitates the use of resources in the classroom and on the computer. Each student has a list of resources available for use in all activities. Jen encourages students to ask each other questions rather than asking her. She also reminds her students that responding with a question can be more helpful than responding with an answer.

At the end of this activity, Jen debriefs with the students in a whole-group format. She collects their work and journals for the purpose of gaining insight into each student's thinking processes and to drive the initial instruction for the following day. Each student also responds on an exit card to one of the following questions: "What tool would a caveman consider to be his most valued possession?" or, "If the Internet is a person's most important tool, what does that statement say about the person's needs?" These questions and responses are used as anticipatory questions to initiate the lesson for the next day.

# DIFFERENTIATED INSTRUCTION: THE 10-STEP PROCESS

Step 1: Examine standards and objectives to be taught. Determine the type of knowledge demanded of the standard and/or objective.

Step 2: Establish the conceptual understanding related to the facts and skills required.

Step 3: For any fact or skill, determine the level of fluency needed for mastery.

Step 4: Design independent student activities that address the facts and skills that are required, along with accommodations for students who need support in achieving mastery of the facts and skills.

Step 5: Reflect on personal knowledge and attitudes related to resources, the content, and the students.

Step 6: Preassess students in knowledge of facts, skills, conceptual understandings, experiences, attitudes, motivations, and ideas.

Step 7: Determine strategies for instruction at different levels of cognitive processing to include concrete, representational, and abstract processes.

**Step 8: Determine the flow of classroom activities to include individual, small-group, and whole-group instruction.**

Step 9: Determine benchmarks of student performance, and develop tools for ongoing measurement of progress.

Step 10: Develop selections and criteria for the summative product or performance that accurately reflect the intended outcomes of the unit.

## SUMMARY

Whole-group instruction, small-group instruction, and individualized instruction are all components of differentiated instruction. Within each format, strategies are available in order to meet the needs of different students. During whole-group instruction, adjustments can be made to the presentation and the environment to support learners. In small-group instruction, the focus is on the systematic rationale for grouping students in order to best meet their needs. During individualized instruction, providing choices to students in relation to how they learn, the materials they use, or how they demonstrate understanding honors differences. Each mode of instruction offers opportunities to provide tailored accommodations matched to learners' needs.

# 8

## *Formative Assessment and the Continuous Monitoring of Progress*

*It is not our differences that divide us. It is our inability to recognize, accept, and celebrate those differences.*

—Audre Lorde, poet

## MEASURING RATE AND DEPTH OF LEARNING

Throughout the instructional process, it is critical to continuously assess the learning of students. While preassessment is critical to the initial stages of differentiation, indicators of progress during the learning are essential to maintain differentiated instruction. Students will receive information in different ways and will internalize their learning at different rates. Instruction must continuously check student progress to include what the students are learning and how quickly they are achieving success. By doing so, it is also possible to identify roadblocks or obstacles a student may be facing in the process. This can then be addressed immediately rather than after instruction has been completed. This ongoing assessment for the purpose of instructional decision making is often referred to as *formative assessment*.

During the learning and teaching process, there are several indicators for monitoring students. These monitoring strategies are often informal in nature, and the sole purpose of the assessment is to drive instruction. There are many factors that affect each student's learning on a daily basis, so it is important to repeat these assessments frequently. It is important to take into account the learner's state at all times. It is best not to wait until the end of instruction to see if students are learning or understanding. The indicators to be monitored can be grouped into three main areas. Monitoring takes place in the areas of the learner's state, the environment, and the learning process itself. While differentiated instruction can be planned ahead of time for the stages of instruction, this monitoring requires the teacher to make constant adjustments throughout the students' learning processes. These adjustments are the responses to the students themselves, and, while some can be predicted, many are instructional decisions made to best meet the students' needs at a given time on a given learning task.

## THE LEARNER'S PHYSICAL STATE

The learner's state of being includes all the physical and mental aspects that affect student learning. These factors determine the readiness of a student to learn new material.

---

The following questions concern aspects related to the physical state of the learner:

Have the student's physical human needs been met?

Has the student's need for sleep been compromised?

Is the student taking medication that affects behavior, fatigue levels, or attention?

Has the student received any needed medication?

Is the student experiencing physical pain?

Does the student have the space needed for a comfortable learning environment?

Is the student overly sensitive to light, noise, or touch?

Is the student in a good physical location to access instruction?

Does the student have the learning materials needed?

At the physical level, there are many issues that a teacher cannot control. However, even the factors that cannot be controlled must be considered during the learning process. For instance, a student who needs medication but has not received it will need a different approach to instruction and learning than if that student had received the needed medication. While a teacher cannot control a student's medication intake, the teacher can respond to the situation by changing approaches to the learning for that student.

## THE LEARNER'S MENTAL STATE

When thinking about the learner's mental state, it is apparent that one aspect must include the student's ability to understand and process concepts related to the desired learner outcome. Beyond the cognitive ability however, there are aspects influenced by emotion and self-concept that must also be considered. Imagine a student who comes to class right after being belittled by an adult in front of peers. This student will not be in a strong state of mind to learn new material. Both the student's cognitive ability and emotional state influence learning. The student's innate abilities along with this emotional state can create, for the teacher, a sense of the student's self-concept as well as an expectation on the part of the teacher of how well the student will perform in class. Students' expectations of themselves also have a tremendous impact on the learning process. Thus, monitoring in relation to the mental state includes assessing cognitive ability as well as perceived ability by both the student and the teacher.

Some questions to ask about the learner:

Are there family issues or social issues distracting the student?

Does this student believe he or she can be successful?

Does the teacher believe the student can be successful?

Is the student clear on the outcomes?

Does the student live in an environment of stress or poverty?

Is the student motivated to succeed?

Is there a motivation to learn built into the learning process?

The factors regarding the learner's state are sometimes apparent and other times are easy to overlook. The questions related to the learner's state are often acknowledged intentionally or instinctively as the student walks into the classroom. There is no need for a formal survey or assessment. This is part of knowing the students. This acknowledgment of the state of the learner is one of the greatest strengths of a teacher and is one of the important human factors of teaching.

## THE ENVIRONMENT

Ongoing monitoring includes an awareness of the conditions in the environment. The environment has a great impact on student learning. Like the learner's state of being, the environment is a factor that is assessed informally and continuously. An awareness of environmental conditions and an understanding of the effect of these factors on student learning are skills that teachers develop and practice without much cognitive processing. For instance, a teacher may acknowledge that an assembly, pep rally, or fire drill is going to affect the attention of the students. Therefore, that teacher adjusts the instruction accordingly. Factors related to the environment include students' perceived safety and the climate within the classroom in relation to risk taking, acceptance, and respect toward learning.

Students need to feel safe in order to learn. Personal safety is a need, and learning is not accomplished efficiently when there is threat to personal safety. The threat may be in the form of physical danger or peer or social danger. Students need to feel safe physically and in their efforts to learn. A student may not risk learning new material if it could result in a humiliating experience. A classroom in which differentiated instruction is practiced honors students performing at different levels. An acceptance of differences and a celebration of those differences make the classroom a better place to be. This type of environment welcomes questions and accepts mistakes as part of the learning process.

## THE LEARNING PROCESS

Progress monitoring in relation to differentiated instruction most often focuses on the learning process itself. There is an emphasis on ongoing, frequent assessment in relation to the student's performance. These formative measures are related to the student's reaction to the material, to the rate of learning, and to the accuracy of that learning. Progress monitoring in this format provides immediate information regarding the response to instruction. This, in turn, directs the next step in the learning process. Differentiated instruction becomes the varied responses to those measures.

# ACCOMMODATIONS

In response to an assessment measure, some students may reflect the need for more support than originally intended or planned. These supports may be needed to assist the learning for struggling students or to provide additional challenge to a student who quickly masters the learning objective. Both of these adjustments to the learning process are accommodations. Accommodations include changes to how a student learns, what materials the student uses to learn, the amount of time provided for the learning, and the tools used to assess the student. Each of these areas of accommodations can be considered when adjusting the learning. The most common adjustments made during the learning process in response to formative assessments are adjustments to the materials used for learning, the time for learning to take place, and the intensity or depth of the topic.

Tiered instructional planning is a strategy used to prepare for the results of formative assessments. In most cases, there will be some students who will struggle with the learning objectives, some who will be on track, and others who will have mastered the objective with little or no instruction. Tiered instructional planning is a format to consider these differences and prepare to react to the learners' performances on the ongoing assessment.

After first considering the desired learning objective and the assessment related to the learning, the instruction is planned for the whole group of students. Then, consideration is made for adjustments to the instruction for students who may struggle and those who may already exceed the learning objective. One aspect of the strength of the tiered instructional-planning format is that there is consideration for students who are at mastery. There are often adjustments and supports made for students who are struggling, but many times higher performing students are left to find their own challenges. This approach considers these learners as well.

As seen in Figure 8.1, the formative assessment is the incremental check to measure the student's ability to complete the learning outcome. The assessment is not necessarily an assessment reflecting mastery of an entire unit or concept. The accommodations on either side of the whole-group learning activity are possible ways to support learners who will need differentiation in order to continue to grow.

Adjustments made for students who have already mastered the material are often more difficult to develop. The adjustment should not simply create additional work for the student but should be something different. The two areas of consideration for those adjustments include providing enrichment opportunities or acceleration opportunities. Enrichment includes increasing either the depth or breadth of the learning objective or changing the level of complexity. Acceleration addresses the rate at which the learning takes place and the pace at which learning occurs.

Enrichment opportunities allow for a student to investigate an area more deeply. Enrichment pushes students to stretch their thinking by using

**Figure 8.1**    Tiered Instructional Planning

| 1. Desired learning outcome: | | |
|---|---|---|
| 2. Formative assessment: | | |
| 4a. Supports or accommodations to be provided for struggling learners | 3. Learning activity or instruction for whole group or on-level learners | 4b. Adjustments to increase the rigor or intensity of the learning for additional challenge |

| Example: | | |
|---|---|---|
| **1. Desired learning outcome:** Students will use transitional words indicating order and organization in writing, to include words such as *first, then, finally, however,* etc. | | |
| **2. Formative assessment:** Students will be asked to identify the words within their writing that show organization and order and to identify order and organizational words in a peer's work | | |
| **4a. Supports:**<br><br>• Students will be provided with index cards or sticky notes to organize steps by writing one card for each step.<br>• Some students may be provided with a topic if needed.<br>• Students may dictate first into a recorder and then write it out. | **3. Learning activity:**<br><br>• Students will write three paragraphs to a younger audience instructing the reader to complete a task with at least 5 steps. | **4b. Adjustments to increase the rigor or intensity:**<br><br>• Students will be asked to write the directions for the task as if the reader was only three inches tall.<br>• Students may be provided with a word bank of higher-level vocabulary to incorporate into the writing. |

critical and creative processes. It encourages students to seek relationships, patterns, trends, and changes. Referring back to Hilda Taba's levels of knowledge (see Tomlinson, 2002), enrichment provides for students to explore the highest levels of knowledge, which go beyond conceptual understandings to include cognition of generalizations and principles.

Acceleration opportunities allow for a student who has mastered a learning objective to move on to the next learning objective without waiting for the class. Acceleration allows for students to move at a faster rate of learning than the whole class. When a formative assessment reflects mastery of a given learning outcome, the student is provided with the next learning outcome to master rather than waiting for the majority of the class to also master the current learning outcome. These adjustments to pacing can be done by collaborating with other professionals to create groups of students who all have this need for additional challenge. It can also be done through many other formats, such as small-group instruction, monitored and supported independent studies, and mentoring.

# JEN'S USE OF ONGOING FORMATIVE ASSESSMENT

Let's take a look at how Jen uses formative assessment and her tiered instructional planning to respond to student needs and adjust her instruction.

It is science class, and the students have been looking at the life cycle of a frog. The objective is for the students to see these changes over time because part of the unit will require students to understand changes and adaptations needed for survival. Today, the students are describing the stages and characteristics of the life cycle of a frog. Jen has incorporated a writing objective by focusing on transitional words showing time passage as well. Before students begin their independent work on this task, Jen gives each student a card and asks them to write their name on it and to simply list the stages of the frog's life cycle that they will be describing. She collects these and quickly looks them over while students are getting materials out. She creates two piles: correct and incorrect. She has five students who have omitted one or more stages on their card. She goes to each of these students and tells them to correct their card before beginning their work. Two students know right away what was missing from the list. Two other students consult resources, and the fifth student needs direct guidance from Jen and the book to identify the missing stage. In a matter of 3 minutes, Jen is sure that all of the students know the names of the stages and the order in which they occur. Now, they can begin the description of each stage with a focus on developmental characteristics.

While Jen's students are working on their independent work, she sees AJ doing little to no work. He is looking around, has sharpened his pencil, changed papers three times, and has still not begun to work. Jen knows he does not like academic tasks. She approaches him and lets him know that she has an expectation that he complete the assignment. She asks if he is clear on what he needs to do. He says yes, he is clear but then says he doesn't "get it." Jen recognizes that AJ's words indicate that he is not clear. She re-explains the assignment, and then, knowing his feelings about writing, asks if it would help him to create a storyboard with captions on the computer rather than handwriting the sequence of events. He agrees to this. Before Jen leaves him, she asks if he has a starting point. He says he does not, so Jen suggests one with which she knows he is familiar.

Jen next notices that Aidan, who has been identified as gifted, is also sitting and doing nothing. She asks him why he is not completing his work and he tells Jen that the assignment is stupid and that he can already do it, "So why should I write it?" Since Jen had prepared her tiered planning template, she is prepared to add additional depth to Aidan's work. The objective was to describe the life cycle of a frog. She tells Aidan since he can already do the objective, she would like him to compare and contrast the life cycle of a frog to the life cycle of a turtle. She states that he should not write more than the other students so he needs to choose his words carefully.

Emily, who is easily distracted, hears what Aidan is doing and asks if she can do the same thing. Emily is also bright and capable as well as creative. Because Emily is going to be missing instruction for vacation, Jen is hesitant to have her do something different from the class so she offers Emily extra credit to create a poster of the differences while she is on vacation. Jen decides she will allow all of her students that opportunity as well.

During the time Jen has these conversations with students, she is keeping an eye on Melissa, Shauna, and Brianna. This morning, Jen knows that Shauna and Brianna were arguing about who was a better friend of Melissa. Jen had already seen Shauna glaring at Brianna earlier in the day. Rather than get into the social mess of 10-year-old girls, Jen simply asks Brianna if she would prefer to work at the back table to get her work done. This way, Shauna cannot make eye contact with her. Brianna looks relieved and gathers her materials to move.

Because Jen knew that Lillie, who was still learning the basics of English, would struggle with the independent work, Jen had already given her a word bank in English with the Spanish equivalent next to it. Lillie was able to use this to complete her work independently. Lillie also knew she had permission to ask Maria for help with vocabulary if needed during science class.

Jen also provided a word bank, in English only, to Elijah, with the thought that this may make the task easier for him and motivate him to complete the learning activity. He seems to be using the list by crossing off each term as he uses it. At one point, he refers to the word bank and says out loud to himself, "Only four more to go."

At the end of the independent work, Jen again asks students for input. She first asks them to use a scale from 1 to 5 and hold up the number of fingers that correlate to the difficulty of the task. She quickly surveys the room. Then she asks students to write on response boards the number of minutes each student thinks it will take to complete the activity. She does this to see if assigning the completion of the activity for homework is reasonable. By constantly assessing students, Jen is able to meet the needs of her class in many aspects. She uses her own observation as well as a written assessment measure and a self-perception survey. All of these tools assist Jen in making instructional decisions that help her students achieve success with the learning outcomes. The planning that Jen did with her tiered-lesson template prepared her with strategies she needed in order to respond to each of her students. Figure 8.2 shows how Jen prepared herself and her instructional plans.

| Figure 8.2 | Jen's Tiered Instructional Planning |

| **1. Desired learning outcome**: Students will describe the different life stages of a frog using transitional words of passage of time and developmental characteristics of a frog's life cycle |

| **2. Formative assessment**: Students will create an accurate description of each stage of the life cycle of a frog in proper sequential order |

| **4a.** | **3.** | **4b.** |
|---|---|---|
| • Create a story board with diagrams and captions (limited text but must include transitional words)<br>• Provide a word bank | • Students will write paragraphs to describe each stage and may provide diagrams to support their text | • Compare and contrast the frog and turtle |

# RESPONSE TO INTERVENTION

Response to intervention (RtI) is a framework designed to integrate progress monitoring and instructional decisions to maximize student achievement and appropriate behavior for all students. RtI provides a structure and system for determining needed levels of services using effective strategies and strategic interventions, and it provides educational support to all students at increasing levels based on individual needs. This tiered framework of supports and services guides the intensity and nature of interventions provided to students in the areas of academics and behavior as a response to student performance and achievement.

The levels within this framework are based on the concept that all students should receive core instruction and universal behavioral interventions. The model rests in the foundation that approximately 80% of students can and should experience success with the core instruction and behavioral systems in the classroom given quality instruction. This is Tier 1. Most commonly, there are three tiers in the model.

For those other 20% of students from Tier 1 who may need more support in order to be successful, additional effective strategies and strategic interventions are provided. These supports are in addition to the core instruction and are considered Tier 2 interventions. The objective of the Tier 2 services is to provide increased intensity and/or additional time in order for students to make accelerated progress. These struggling students need to make gains at a faster rate to keep from falling further behind. Besides remediation for struggling learners, Tier 2 can also include opportunities for increased depth and complexity for students needing additional challenge.

Finally, there will be a small number of students who do not respond to the strategic interventions or reflect needed growth at the Tier 2 level of support. This may be as few as 5% of all students. These students may require individualized instructional strategies in order to experience success. These intensive supports and services are received in Tier 3. (See Figure 8.3.)

| **Figure 8.3** Response to Intervention Supports and Services | |
|---|---|
| *Tiers of RtI* | *Support and Service* |
| Tier 1<br>100% of students<br>Expectation of about 80% success rate | Core instruction in the classroom for all students and universal behavioral programs |
| Tier 2<br>For those needing supports in addition to Tier 1 for success | All supports and services of Tier 1 plus strategic interventions with progress tracked though frequent progress monitoring |
| Tier 3<br>Very small number of students needing even more services than received through Tier 1 and Tier 2 | All supports and services of Tiers 1 and 2 plus individualized intervention supports and strategies with regular monitoring of progress |

Jen has demonstrated the supports and services available in Tier 1. It includes high-quality curriculum along with supports and accommodations for students. However, there are some students in Jen's class who need more supports than even her quality, differentiated instruction can provide. Both Elijah and AJ receive additional reading instruction from the reading specialist each day. Aidan attends a class for gifted students, and Lillie receives assistance from an English language specialist each week. These services are all Tier 2 interventions. These students receive all the services that Jen can provide, and they receive more intensive instruction as well. In addition, Jen also has two students with IEPs and one with an individualized behavior plan. These students receive services from specialists who are able to provide intensive individualized supports. These individualized supports and services are Tier 3 interventions.

Therefore, the entire premise of the response to intervention model is based on differentiated instructional practices. Students receive supports and services based on their needs. Then, within each tier of the model, differentiation is necessary to implement the supports and services. As the tiers move up, differentiation becomes more systematic and more individualized in nature. While instruction at Tier 1 can be differentiated through a large number of factors, instruction at Tiers 2 and 3 are based specifically on academic or behavioral needs and remediation. Tiers 2 and 3 are specific to the results of diagnostic assessments and regular assessments to measure progress.

# QUESTIONING AS FORMATIVE ASSESSMENT

In order to continuously assess progress and the thought processes of students, questioning must be routine and deliberate. Questions should be strategically developed to provide insight on the rate of learning, the stages of learning, and the level of mastery.

There are at least four purposes or functions of questioning related to monitoring progress. Questions are used to assess (1) accuracy, (2) personal meaning, (3) an understanding of connections or applications, and (4) new questions a student may have. When asking a question for assessment purposes, what you are assessing will be one of these four categories. An assessment question may be to determine a student's level of accuracy: correct, incorrect, or somewhere in between. A question could be for the purpose of discovering what meaning the student has built around a concept either personally or in relation to other understandings. A final purpose for questions of assessment may be to promote a student to ask new questions related to a topic:

Accuracy: "Can you show me the seven continents on a map and name them?"

Personal Meaning: "From what we learned about the lake's ecosystem, how do you feel about allowing waterskiing in the lake?"

Connections or Applications: "How is the ocean like a rainforest? How is it different?"

New Questions: "Now that you know something about Robert Frost and his work, what would you ask him if you could?"

Often, verbs derived from taxonomies are used to develop questions. However, these simply provide a framework for levels of questioning with literal questions being the lowest level of questioning and analytical or evaluative questions being the highest level. Many times, these taxonomies are misrepresented and used inappropriately. The levels of questions should not be used to differentiate instruction by asking struggling students the lower levels of questions and higher performing students the higher-level questions. All students should be challenged with high level questioning. It is a mistake and certainly a disservice to struggling students to always ask them to answer only literal questions. In many cases, these are the same students who struggle most with recall and have an easier time with the conceptual understandings than the isolated facts.

Therefore, if questions are not differentiated by levels of cognitive complexity, they need to be differentiated by the type of processing required. Two broad types of thought processing are critical thinking and creative thinking. Different students may have strengths in either area. Both types of processes have the capacity to demand high levels of questioning. Rather than arranging the verbs from taxonomies in a linear fashion, these verbs can be arranged by these two thought processes. (See Figure 8.4.)

Combining both the purpose of the questioning along with the thinking process provides a new way to arrange questions. The purpose of the questioning can remain the same for all students. However, the type of thought processing demanded can be different for students based on areas of strength. Most important, all students are held accountable for responses to high levels of questioning.

| **Figure 8.4** | Aligning Verbs to Purpose and Thinking Processes |
| --- | --- |

| *Purposes of Questioning* | *Critical Thinking* | *Creative Thinking* |
| --- | --- | --- |
| Accuracy of Information | Appraise, argue, assess, compare, contrast, critique, determine, discriminate, evaluate, infer, judge, justify, plan, prove, scrutinize, structure, validate | Adapt, alter, combine, compose, conclude, generate, hypothesize, interpret, invent, join, modify, predict, reframe, substitute |
| Personal Meaning | | |
| Connections/Applications | | |
| New Questions | | |

For example, the desired outcome is for students to have an understanding of the characteristics of mammals. Questions should be developed to check accuracy of the students' understandings. Following are example questions to check the accuracy of the desired outcome:

A student strong in critical processing can be asked, "How would you prove to me that a dolphin is a mammal?" or, "What determines the category of a mammal from other classes?" A student strong in the creative processes may be asked, "What if a shark breathed air? Would it then be a mammal?" or, "Can you create a fictitious mammal with all the characteristics of a mammal visible?" In math, one student strong in critical thinking skills may be asked to compare the processes of addition and multiplication while a student strong in creative thinking may be asked to create a model to show how addition and multiplication are alike. Both assess the same objective but the questioning is approached differently for different students.

This use of different types of questions no longer limits the depth of reflected understanding and instead provides a way to differentiate questioning. When questioning students for the purpose of measuring the learning progress, rate, or depth of mastery, high-level questions can be asked within an area of strength for each student. If the questioning is designed to check connections of new knowledge to old, a creative student may be asked a "what if" question, while another student may be asked to compare or contrast the new learning to something mastered previously. First, the purpose of the question is determined. What is the aspect of the learning that is being checked? Then, the question is designed based on the processing strength of the student. All students are ensured rigorous, high-level questions.

## DIFFERENTIATED INSTRUCTION: THE 10-STEP PROCESS

Step 1: Examine standards and objectives to be taught. Determine the type of knowledge demanded of the standard and/or objective.

Step 2: Establish the conceptual understanding related to the facts and skills required.

Step 3: For any fact or skill, determine the level of fluency needed for mastery.

Step 4: Design independent student activities that address the facts and skills that are required, along with accommodations for students who need support in achieving mastery of the facts and skills.

Step 5: Reflect on personal knowledge and attitudes related to resources, the content, and the students.

Step 6: Preassess students in knowledge of facts, skills, conceptual understandings, experiences, attitudes, motivations, and ideas.

Step 7: Determine strategies for instruction at different levels of cognitive processing to include concrete, representational, and abstract processes.

Step 8: Determine the flow of classroom activities to include individual, small-group, and whole-group instruction.

**Step 9: Determine benchmarks of student performance, and develop tools for ongoing measurement of progress.**

Step 10: Develop selections and criteria for the summative product or performance that accurately reflect the intended outcomes of the unit.

## SUMMARY

Differentiation and high-quality instruction require ongoing monitoring of student learning. There are many factors that influence student learning, and these factors must be taken into account throughout the learning process. Both the environment and the learner's state impact learning and demand instructional adjustments. These factors are always changing and must be monitored regularly. Student progress must also be continuously assessed through formal and informal measures. These formative assessment practices serve the purpose of driving instruction and illuminating student needs. The RtI model is a three-leveled tier of supports and services based on those student needs. Like all aspects of differentiated instruction, the objective is to meet individual student needs for student success. Formative instruction also requires questioning students to identify levels of mastery or progress. All students should be questioned with high-level questions. Differentiation occurs by tailoring questions to areas of critical or creative thinking based on the student's strength.

# 9

## *Summative Assessments and Products*

*The mediocre teacher tells. The good teacher explains. The superior teacher demonstrates. The great teacher inspires.*

—William Arthur Ward, reading teacher

**B**esides the formative assessments used for ongoing progress monitoring and instructional decision making, there are also cumulative assessments referred to as *summative assessments.* These are assessments or products completed at the culmination of the learning activity or unit to reflect what the student has learned or mastered. In some cases, these assessments may be in the form of traditional pencil-and-paper exams. However, in many cases, the same information can be obtained through the use of products rather than traditional tests. Using both written assessments and products can allow for students to show what they have learned or now know. Both formats can be differentiated to best meet the needs of students.

The purpose of a summative assessment is to provide an opportunity for students to reflect on their own learning, abilities, and understandings. These assessments should not be designed to trick, stump, or catch students making errors. The nature of a summative assessment should be one of support and encouragement. The goal is for students to experience success and have an opportunity to demonstrate their achievement. Therefore, differentiating products and summative assessments are for the purpose of supporting students in their efforts to communicate their knowledge.

## EMPOWERMENT AND CONTRIBUTION

While the purpose of the summative assessment is to provide the opportunity for students to share what they have learned, the motivation for students to do so is also a critical component. As a student reflects on his or her learning, the quality of the communication is dependent on the motivation of the student. Therefore, any summative assessment should be purposeful and intentional for both the teacher and the student. The assessment should be viewed as an opportunity for the student and should be used as a vehicle to empower the student. Different types of assessments and products offer different degrees of possibility for student empowerment. The more the student is involved in determining the direction of the assessment, the more motivated the student will be.

## TYPES OF ASSESSMENTS

Summative assessments can be very different from each other in their formats. The most critical component of the assessment is alignment with the learning objectives. There are many wonderful lists and banks of products and forms available for assessment purposes; however, if the assessment does not match the objective, the product becomes a project as opposed to an assessment tool. The other critical aspect of any summative assessment is its ability to allow a student to accurately show what he or she has learned. A teacher may say, "Andre knew the information yesterday when I discussed it with him, but today he did poorly on the exam." In this case, the teacher should not be using the exam as a summative assessment. Her statement shows that the exam apparently did not allow the student to communicate what he learned. A summative assessment is an indicator of what a student knows, can do, believes, or understands.

## WRITTEN-RESPONSE PRODUCTS

There are two main types of written-response products. They are open-ended and closed-ended responses to a prompt or question. Open-ended questions are favorable in that they provide the potential for a student to accurately demonstrate or share the knowledge he or she has learned. However, because there are so many variables, using open-ended questions for assessment purposes can present obstacles. While closed-ended questions are easy to evaluate, they often limit a student's ability to show what they know. Since the purpose of assessment is just that, closed-ended response questions should be used sparingly and only after considerations of the drawbacks have been made.

## Closed-Ended Assessments

One common type of questioning is the true/false format. There are some drawbacks to consider with this type of assessment tool. These types of statements are difficult to create with no gray area. Often, there will be an exception to a fact. Many of the brightest students struggle with these not because they did not understand the concept but because they did not know how to answer the question due to seeing the gray area. These questions also can mislead students. They often trip up the student who struggles to read the statement the way the statement was intended to be read. Finally, another drawback is the lack of validity to the questioning itself. A student has a 50% chance of guessing a correct answer without even reading the statement. Therefore, this type of assessment does not accurately allow students to show what they know.

Multiple-choice questions are another type of selection-based assessment. These questions are not open ended and have some of the same drawbacks as the true/false questions. An additional drawback to multiple-choice questions is the amount of critical reading required. This assessment tool will often reflect reading ability as much as knowledge of content. If multiple-choice questions are used, there should be straightforward options and not choices that include or exclude multiple options, such as "A and C but not B." This becomes an assessment of reading comprehension as much as any content knowledge.

A third type of closed-ended assessment tool that has several weaknesses is a set of matching terms and definitions. This becomes a poor reflection of knowledge due to the nature of the task. Each response is interdependent on the other responses. If one response is incorrect, other responses are incorrect as well. Therefore, if this type of assessment is used, there should be a small number of items in each matching set. Also, for struggling readers, it is helpful to place the longer stem on the left and the shorter of the pair on the right. This way, the reader needs to read the longer stem only one time and then read through the shorter choices multiple times as opposed to reading a word once and then having to read long definitions multiple times.

| More Difficult for Struggling Readers: | |
|---|---|
| Single word or short phrase here | Long definition or description here |
| More Favorable for Struggling Readers: | |
| Long definition or description here | Single word or short phrase here |

### Open-Ended Assessments

In most cases, the previous types of assessment questions are found in the lower levels of questioning. One way to raise the level of questioning is through open-ended questioning. These pencil-and-paper exams can be adapted to better meet the strengths and needs of learners. There are many accommodations that can be provided to help struggling learners in extended response questions. There are also adaptations that can be provided to challenge gifted learners. Unless writing is the focus of the assessment, the following are some accommodations to support students in communicating their responses:

- Recorded responses
- Presentation through graphics and visuals to support their ideas
- Graphic organizers to help organize thoughts
- Dictation to a scribe
- Use of a computer

## ADAPTATIONS FOR WRITTEN RESPONSES FOR GIFTED LEARNERS

For gifted students, open-ended questions raise issues of their own. In some cases, gifted students may feel if they know the material there is no reason for them to write it all out. For these students, the accommodations provided above may also be appropriate. Other gifted students may feel they need to expand their answer to include everything they know about the topic or in any way related to the topic. The response may have no end. For these students, providing a framework may be helpful. The framework can be as simple as a word bank to indicate the areas of the topic that must be addressed in the response. It could also mean providing limits on the length of responses. It is important to remember that while gifted students may not struggle to master concepts, they still may need accommodations and differentiation as well.

There are several experts in the field of the development of curriculum for gifted students. Each provides suggestions and strategies for differentiating the assignments and assessments for learners who are gifted. Generally speaking, there are some commonalities among the leaders in the field. When addressing the needs of students identified as gifted, one approach is to use one of these common accommodations:

- Expanding meaning by connecting to other studies
- Exploring from a new or different perspective
- Changing an element of the situation, task, or environment
- Generating new possibilities
- Evaluating the content or concept

These can be used as helpful considerations when adapting material for students who have already mastered the concepts or skills. Rather than assigning the student a task that he or she has already mastered, or assigning him or her more work than other students, these five bullets can provide guidance in adjusting the assignment to add more complexity. Using any one of these five areas also allows for assignments to be differentiated rather than assignments that are totally different than the other students. Following are some examples of how an open-ended response question can be posed to students on level and then adjusted for students achieving above performance expectations.

---

### Examples of Elements to Differentiate Questions for Gifted and High-Achieving Learners

#### Connections to Expand Meaning

For on-level learners: What leadership traits did the main character in the story demonstrate?

For learners who are gifted or high performing: How were the leadership traits of the main character like those of the current president?

#### Exploration With a New Perspective

For on-level learners: How was the villain in the story responsible for the collapse of the community?

For learners who are gifted or high performing: How could you defend or explain the actions of the villain in the story?

#### Change of an Element

For on-level learners: How does boiling the solution change its density? Explain.

For learners who are gifted or high performing: How would the density be different when boiled if the compound had more oxygen in it?

#### Exploration of New Possibilities

For on-level learners: How did the time period in which the story was set affect the plot?

For learners who are gifted or high performing: How would the plot be affected if the story took place 500 years later?

#### Evaluation

For on-level learners: What are the most important products that should be recycled and why?

For learners who are gifted or high performing: When does recycling go too far? Explain.

These examples show how differentiation can occur by changing the direction of the question rather than providing a completely different task. In both cases, there are higher-level questions. In each pair of questions, the question does not require more work to answer, but it does require deeper thinking.

## PROBLEM-BASED PRODUCTS

Beyond simply using traditional means to assess students, problem-based products are a more authentic way for students to communicate what they know. Through the creation or identification of a problem, students must apply their learning to a situation. The situation may be real, fictitious, on paper, or requiring practice or action. No matter how the question is presented, problem-based products present a scenario that the student must address and communicate or demonstrate the solution or steps toward a solution.

Problem-based questions must be constructed carefully in order to fully align with the objectives. The question needs to be directly related to the desired learning outcome. If it is not aligned, the problem becomes an exercise of problem solving for its own value and not for the use of assessment. Problem solving on its own is valuable, but if the purpose is to provide an opportunity for students to communicate what they know or can do related to a desired outcome, the problem-solving process must be aligned to that outcome. Because students are not limited to a single correct answer or certain perspective, the direction of the solution can become highly unpredictable.

In order to contain responses to reflect the desired learning outcomes, it is important to provide guidance or intentionally frame the question. Providing a description of the expectation or requirements of the solution up front allows students flexibility in their thinking while remaining on track with the desired outcome. For instance, the question asks students to measure the height of a building using a barometer, and the prompt includes that the student must find at least two ways to solve the problem. This leaves the responses open yet communicates the expectation that there must be at least two solutions. Another way to frame this type of response is by providing specific requirements. This can be done through the use of descriptors, elements to be considered, or even specific terms that must be used. Using the problem stated above of measuring the height of a building using a barometer, students may be instructed that an acceptable solution requires the use of a principle of physics to solve the problem. This is stated to the students along with the problem itself. Finally, the question can be posed in conjunction with a desired outcome. The student has the starting and ending point and must work out how to arrive at the outcome. Using the barometer question again, students may be asked, "How did I discover that the building was 410 feet high with only a barometer?"

# PERFORMANCE-BASED PRODUCTS

Related to problem-based assessments are performance-based products. Performance-based products require students to create a product to reflect learning. Unlike problem-based assessments, well-designed performance-based assessments are more often authentic practices or actions and rarely involve fictitious scenarios. They are also rarely completed on paper as opposed to the problem-based assessments, which may or may not be. Performance-based products require many of the same frameworks and conditions as problem-based assessments. Providing clear expectations, requirements, or restrictions must be done clearly and up front. There are many resources in both books and Web sites that provide hundreds of student products. These list everything from designing a brochure, to creating a puppet, to developing a PowerPoint presentation. The caution here is that it is very easy to use these lists as a menu and simply select different products that students may enjoy. These products quickly become fun products for students without reflecting any evidence of the desired learning objective. For instance, creating a puppet to represent a historic figure may be fun and will reflect the student's perception of the appearance of the person. However, if the objective is for students to identify and relate to characteristics of leadership, creating a puppet of a president does not align to the objective. Therefore, when using product-based assessments, it important to continually reflect on the desired learning objective and its alignment to the assessment product.

One of the strengths of performance-based products is that this assessment lends itself to an authentic task. Students are able to take action, create something, or do something in response to the prompt. The best performance-based assessments also allow for authentic audiences who have some interest in the contribution or work of the student. This becomes both a powerful motivator and an important learning experience. The student is able to make connections and take actions to solve real-world problems. In some cases, this affords opportunities for a student to practice as a professional in a field of study, complete a case study, or make a meaningful contribution through service learning. At the very least, it allows for students to not only communicate their knowledge and understandings but to also practice new skills, act on new knowledge, and challenge existing knowledge.

# AFFECTIVE PRODUCTS

A final area of assessment is through the use of affective products. These products get to the heart of the learner. Affective products require reflection by the learner. They foster powerful intrapersonal experiences, allowing for a student to interact with new knowledge and process its personal meaning. This can be a very deep level of learning as the student reflects back on how the learning experience, new knowledge, or understandings have changed him or her as a person. These assessments address the intrapersonal aspects of learning and contribute to developing the skills of a lifelong learner. Journaling and personal response is one form of an affective product. There are many other creative ways in which a student can express what the learning means in a personal sense. Public speaking, teaching another person, writing, or describing a new passion are all ways in which these products can be used to assess a student.

## USING RUBRICS TO COMMUNICATE EXPECTATIONS

One of the most important aspects of open-ended assessments is the importance of communicating the expectations up front. Students should know what aspects of the question or product they are being assessed on and to what degree each aspect rates in importance. It must be remembered that the grade of the assessment is not the focal point. The communication of knowledge and skills gained is the focus of any summative assessment. Therefore, in order for students to communicate their learning effectively, they need to be provided with a lens through which to reflect that learning.

Rubrics make clear the expectations and level of performance or product that is considered acceptable, less than acceptable, and beyond expectations. Rubrics are vehicles to communicate expectations beforehand as well as the product or performance assessment afterward. Rubrics specify the critical components of a product along with levels of quality or mastery. Levels of mastery as indicated by defined criteria set the stage for student success. Rubrics are shared with students before instruction. The learner, trying to communicate ideas and new learning, must be clear on what is to be expected and how to communicate in a way that matches the perspective of the audience. Therefore, rubrics can be an effective tool to help students plan and implement their own products and performances.

Well-designed rubrics provide a communication tool about assessment to both students and parents. Rubrics can be developed with input from the learner. Rubrics designed by the teacher collaboratively with the learner provide buy in, motivation, and clarity. Once the aspects of the product have been made clear, along with the levels of degree of quality for each aspect, the rubric can be used to compare with the student product or performance. The rubric becomes a tool for summative assessment. This tool identifies, through the assessment, the areas of strength and weakness of a particular product. Conversations regarding the levels of quality or mastery are beneficial to all involved.

Rubrics can be as simple as a three-point rubric on a single aspect of a product, or they can have multiple levels of quality indicators in multiple areas. Designing a rubric requires thought regarding the components and/or subskills of a particular performance or product. After determining the different components involved, the next step is to determine the levels of performance or mastery expected at the highest level. This is described and is assigned to the highest point value on the rubric. That description is then considered for the purpose of determining which characteristics may be missing, inaccurate, or of lesser quality from the product. That level is then described and assigned to the next lowest level on the point scale. At the bottom level of the rubric is a descriptor of an unacceptable product or performance that would earn zero points. Here is a simple rubric to illustrate this design:

---

Objective: Students will identify the main parts of a plant on a diagram and describe the purpose of each part.

3 points: The student labels the six parts of a plant and defines each part accurately.

2 points: The student labels four or more parts of a plant and defines three to five parts accurately.

1 point: The student labels four to six parts of a plant and defines zero to two parts accurately.

0 points: The student labels zero to three parts of a plant and defines less than three parts accurately.

---

More complex rubrics may have up to six points possible and may have several qualifiers or descriptors for each level. When developing rubrics, the desired learning objectives must be at the heart of the development. Assessing a poster depicting the parts of a plant should more likely focus around the accuracy of the plant parts rather than the lettering of the poster's title. However, if the poster is also part of a media study, then maybe the lettering of the title becomes much more important. It is essential to be clear on the objective before creating a rubric to be used for assessment.

## TYPES OF KNOWLEDGE ASSESSED AND MATCHED TO PRODUCTS

When selecting the type of assessment or product to use for summative assessment, it may help to consider the type of knowledge being assessed. Taba's types of knowledge (see Tomlinson et al., 2001) can again be used here. It only makes sense that the instructional decisions are made by the

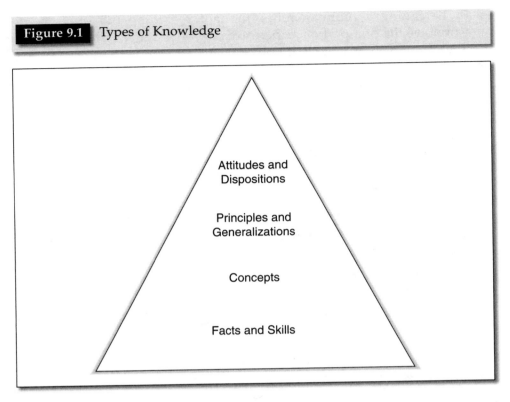

Figure 9.1    Types of Knowledge

Attitudes and
Dispositions

Principles and
Generalizations

Concepts

Facts and Skills

same underlying decisions as the assessment. Therefore, looking at the types of knowledge can provide insight into rationale for selecting assessments. (See Figure 9.1.)

Most of the closed-ended types of assessments including true-false items, multiple-choice questions, and matching sets assess the basic type of knowledge. They assess facts and skills. The questions and answers are generally correct or incorrect with little gray area. When assessing facts and skills, these forms of summative assessment may be appropriate. However, when assessing concepts, students need to be able to express ideas and new learning in a less restricted format. Open-ended, extended-response questions are more likely to provide a format that lends itself to allowing students to communicate more thoroughly and accurately. In order for students to communicate new learning of generalizations and principles or new attitudes and dispositions, students must have the opportunity to apply and transfer their learning. Therefore, problem- and performance-based products along with affective-based products, which are products that center on intrapersonal skills, are more appropriate choices for assessment.

An assessment to reflect learning of addition facts may be in a multiple-choice format. An assessment to reflect a student's understanding of the relationship between the seasons and the Earth's movement will require a more open format, such as an extended response or product. An assessment to reflect new attitudes and values regarding overseas trade will require a product, performance, or affective product, such as a reflection journal to indicate new learning.

## Jen's Use of Summative Assessments and Products

During the year, Jen's students studied the Civil War with a focus on how conflict can lead to positive progress. Students studied the changes that took place during and after the war in relation to the economics of the country, the political nature of the country as a whole, transportation, communication, and inventions. These factors, in turn, changed the lifestyles of many people. At the end of the unit, Jen wanted to know what her students had learned. She had many facts and skills that she wanted to assess. She also had many related concepts she wanted the students to grasp as well as the big idea that conflict creates change, and in this case, progress.

Jen went back to her original unit plan to examine her unit's desired learning outcomes. For each of these, she had identified the type of knowledge inherent to the learning. This became her guide to consider assessment tools.

She then looked at each of her facts and skills. Many of the facts were historical facts and vocabulary. She had also included some geography skills in the unit. In order to assess these, Jen selected to use a closed-ended pencil-and-paper assessment. She designed some multiple-choice questions and some cloze sentences with a word bank containing six words. Jen also included a short activity in which students had to use their map skills to identify locations on a map. In all, there were 20 questions. When the time came for students to complete this assessment, she offered to read orally to any students who preferred that accommodation. About six students chose to take advantage of that support. Jen also allowed Lillie to have any assessment items translated if she needed translations. However, for the vocabulary, she did not allow Lillie to have the vocabulary words translated because the objective was for students to know the vocabulary terms in English. Jen also separated the assessment into three different pages for AJ so that he could complete one section at a time and see his progress. She had discovered earlier in the year that this kept him from rushing through to be the first one done.

Another interesting observation was Jen's consideration when Julia took this assessment. Jen learned that the night before this assessment Julia's brother had a birthday party and Julia was up until after midnight with a new puppy. Julia was tired, complaining of a headache, and unfocused. Jen knew that Julia knew the material but would not do well on the day of the assessment. Jen allowed Julia to read a book quietly while students took the assessment if Julia agreed that she would complete the assessment the following day during her free time or during lunch. Jen knew that Julia would not be able to accurately communicate what she knew about the facts and skills being assessed, so she was willing to provide a more opportune time for Julia to communicate her learning.

Jen was also concerned about assessing the students on their conceptual understandings of conflict and positive progress. Therefore, she chose to assign a product-based assessment to allow students to communicate what they had learned throughout the unit. Jen wanted to allow the students to have some choice in their products, but she also wanted parameters. She carefully designed her assessment so that she could provide choice as well as communicate expectations while allowing students to select an area of strength to communicate their learning. Following is the assessment that Jen created.

## End-of-Unit Assessment on Conflict and Change

You are nearing the completion of the unit designed to teach about conflict and its effects on a variety of elements in a culture, society, and country. In your studies about the Civil War, you learned about a historical conflict and the many outcomes of that war. Now is the time to highlight what you have learned.

Your job is to create a product that reflects how the Civil War created lasting change. We have examined the workforce, inventions, the economy, transportation, and communication to name a few. The change may be in any area you choose. You will create a cause-effect visual to show what changes occurred in your selected field as a result of the Civil War. You will also create a fictitious cause-effect visual to show what changes would not have taken place or what life would be like in your selected field had there not been a war.

Here are the criteria for the first visual:

- The chart must be easy to read and done neatly. It will be displayed in the school.
- The chart must be labeled and communicate at least four significant changes that occurred. A significant change is one that lasted through time and either still exists or evolved into something more modern.
- The chart must provide information communicating how or why the conflict forced this change. What need or desire was met by the change?

Here are the criteria for the second:

- The chart must be easy to read and done neatly.
- The chart must be labeled and communicate at least four significant changes that would not have occurred had there been no war.
- The chart must provide information communicating, if the change did not occur, what need or desire would not have existed or been met?

After completing the cause-effect product, you will create a second product to demonstrate your knowledge of a conflict of your choice (other than the Civil War) and how that conflict produced positive changes. This conflict may be personal, within the community, or on a national scale. It must be a true conflict. This product can be in any format of your choice. You may choose to use technology, create something artistic, journal entries, an essay, or even a performance of some kind. The rubric provided shows elements to consider.

| Figure 9.2 | Rubric for Product Assessment on Conflict and Change |

| Points | Descriptive criteria |
|---|---|
| 6 | • The chosen conflict is a real conflict.<br>• Outcomes of the conflict are clearly positive in nature.<br>• Negative outcomes are addressed and discounted as being less significant than the positive ones.<br>• There are at least six positive outcomes communicated as directly linked to the conflict.<br>• Product is the quality of a school or community performance or display.<br>• Product is created in an area of personal strength and is appropriate for an audience of peers and adults.<br>• A self-assessment reflection is completed after the product is complete with both strengths and possible changes. |
| 5 | • The chosen conflict is a real conflict.<br>• Outcomes of the conflict are positive in nature.<br>• Negative outcomes are addressed and discounted as being less significant than the positive ones.<br>• There are five positive outcomes communicated as directly linked to the conflict.<br>• Product is the quality of a classroom or school performance or display.<br>• Product is created in an area of personal strength and is appropriate for an audience of peers and adults. |
| 4 | • The chosen conflict is a real conflict.<br>• Outcomes of the conflict are positive in nature.<br>• Negative outcomes are addressed.<br>• There are fewer than five positive outcomes communicated as linked to the conflict.<br>• Product is the quality of a classroom performance or display.<br>• Product is created in an area of personal strength and is appropriate for an audience of peers. |
| 3 | • The chosen conflict is a real conflict.<br>• Outcomes of the conflict are fairly positive in nature.<br>• There are fewer than five outcomes communicated as loosely related to the conflict.<br>• Product is the quality of a classroom display.<br>• Product is appropriate for an audience of peers. |
| 2 | • The chosen conflict is a real conflict.<br>• Outcomes of the conflict are not clearly linked to the conflict.<br>• There are fewer than five outcomes communicated.<br>• Product is the quality of a classroom display.<br>• Product is appropriate for an audience of peers. |

*(Continued)*

**Figure 9.2** (Continued)

| Points | Descriptive criteria |
|--------|---------------------|
| 1 | • The chosen conflict is a real conflict.<br>• Outcomes of the conflict are not clearly linked to the conflict.<br>• There are fewer than five positive outcomes communicated.<br>• Product is not at a quality ready for display.<br>• Product is not appropriate for an audience of peers. |
| 0 | • The conflict is not real.<br>• There are no clear outcomes related to the conflict. |

Jen provided this rubric along with the assignment and due date. (See Figure 9.2.) She also posted the rubric on a wall in a place where students could easily refer to the criteria, and she sent a copy of it home so parents could see it as well. Jen understood the importance of students understanding the expectations of the assessment. Her goal was to provide a format for students to communicate their learning. She provided choice and encouraged them to capitalize on an area of strength rather than giving them a one-size-fits-all assessment. Jen's students were motivated by their decision-making power. By using both choice and product-based assessments, Jen avoided parents completing the work for their children, as the students wanted to create their own products.

During the time students worked on their products, Jen provided accommodations to students. She had individual conferences with each student to clarify the assignment and guide students in the planning of their products. For several students, Jen assisted in the creation of a schedule so that they could complete their products on time. Throughout the entire year, Jen spent time discussing quality so that students were clear as to the definitions of *community, school,* and *classroom quality.* There was an entirely separate rubric regarding quality of work to be displayed with which students were familiar. This was posted in the classroom and was part of the class culture.

## DIFFERENTIATED INSTRUCTION: THE 10-STEP PROCESS

Step 1: Examine standards and objectives to be taught. Determine the type of knowledge demanded of the standard and/or objective.

Step 2: Establish the conceptual understanding related to the facts and skills required.

Step 3: For any fact or skill, determine the level of fluency needed for mastery.

Step 4: Design independent student activities that address the facts and skills that are required, along with accommodations for students who need support in achieving mastery of the facts and skills.

Step 5: Reflect on personal knowledge and attitudes related to resources, the content, and the students.

Step 6: Preassess students in knowledge of facts, skills, conceptual understandings, experiences, attitudes, motivations, and ideas.

Step 7: Determine strategies for instruction at different levels of cognitive processing to include concrete, representational, and abstract processes.

Step 8: Determine the flow of classroom activities to include individual, small-group, and whole-group instruction.

Step 9: Determine benchmarks of student performance, and develop tools for ongoing measurement of progress.

**Step 10: Develop selections and criteria for the summative product or performance that accurately reflect the intended outcomes of the unit.**

## SUMMARY

The purpose of summative assessment is for students to communicate their learning. With that in mind, there are several closed-ended assessments that provide a format for students to display facts and skills they have learned. There are limitations to closed-ended responses, however. In order for students to communicate conceptual learning, open-ended assessments provide more options. While there are several options for summative assessments, the decision as to which to use should be based on both the type of knowledge being assessed as well as the format that best allows students to communicate their learning. Expectations for any assessment should be clearly stated up front. Rubrics provide guidance to students as well as function as a communication tool in the assessment process.

# 10

## *Wrap-Up and Final Thoughts*

*Share our similarities. Celebrate our differences.*

—M. Scott Peck, author

## PRACTICE FOR NEW HABITS

The 10-step process of differentiating instruction is in-depth and rigorous. Each and every one of the steps requires careful planning and forethought. In order to implement these 10 steps, adequate time must be provided for learning, analyzing, and planning. While, still all too often, time is the greatest commodity for teachers, there needs to be a strong message about this need for time to study, prepare, collaborate, and develop lesson plans. Instruction is only as good as the preparation. In order to move forward with this process using what time can be afforded, here are some suggestions to make this process more manageable.

A practice that requires time and yet reaps benefits far greater than its demands is the practice of collaboration. Working with other professionals in the field allows professionals to share ideas, resources, and knowledge. Rich conversations, professional growth, and new ideas are all developed by collaborating. The questions for collaboration in the Appendix promote this practice. By sharing, we lighten the load and increase the wealth.

A recommendation for practice is to select one of the 10 steps of the differentiation process and continuously focus on the elements involved with that one specific step during a particular instructional unit. While each of the steps of the process is important and should be given attention, one may be chosen as a special interest. For instance, a teacher may choose to be acutely aware of preassessments and examine the selection of the preassessments as well as the indicators from the preassessment.

When an instructor selects a single step in the process, and deeply examines the practices of that step, not only will that particular instructional skill be improved but simultaneously the overall instruction will be improved. In addition, the professional development will expand exponentially. Not only will the practices within the particular unit of study become more refined, other units and instructional experiences will improve as well. As deep learning occurs, new habits of mind are formed. These new thoughts and practices will transfer to other opportunities. As this happens, the practices will become more natural and fluid. While it may be very deliberate at first to consider how products align with the learning outcome within a particular science unit, for example, with practice, the question of alignment between products and objectives will become second nature in all areas of instruction.

## SYSTEMATIC, INTENTIONAL INSTRUCTION

Throughout the discussion of each of the 10 steps, there have been two common factors for each. The first factor is that each of the 10 steps requires intentionality. It has been clear that each step is explicitly defined within itself and within the system as a whole. Nothing here is about making teaching decisions based on gut feelings. There are no random acts of instruction. Each instructional decision is made based on valid information. These 10 steps and their related elements are the science of teaching. Each step is systematic and intentional. The 10 steps are the structure for instruction.

The second common trait, and equally important within each of the 10 steps, is that the actual practices within the 10 steps define the art of teaching. While implementing any one of the 10 steps, there is no recipe that works every time. There are no hard-and-fast decisions or rules. Differentiated instruction is not black and white. While there are 10 distinct steps listed, the differentiation of instruction is not a checklist. The decisions made within each of these steps are fluid and changing. The conditions in which they are made are also never the same twice. Responding to this becomes the art of teaching that each professional brings to the system.

These two common elements bring forth the challenge and excitement of differentiated instruction. It is the blending of art and science. While there are deliberate and systematic actions and instructional decisions, these actions and decisions are set with different parameters every time.

Differentiating instruction cannot be a cut-and-paste process. Because it is responsive in nature, it is ever changing, even within its own system.

## STUDENTS WITH SPECIAL NEEDS

There has been a great deal of focus on the instructional process with little mention about particular groups of students. Differentiated instruction is student centered. It begins and ends with the student. It does not matter who the student is or what label the student may or may not have. Differentiated instruction is appropriate for all learners. Age levels, performance levels, race, gender, and economic levels are not factors that determine the value of differentiated instruction.

There has been some misconception regarding the relationship between differentiated instruction and students with special needs. There should be no misunderstanding here because all students benefit from differentiated instruction. Differentiated instruction is not limited to minor adaptations within any one of these steps. It includes all the actions done as a response to what the student needs in order to be successful. No child needs to be sent to another room or to another teacher in order to receive a differentiated curriculum. While those may be additional supports for a student to be successful, those decisions are made based on the instruction and student need and not simply as a replacement to the differentiated instruction that occurs within the child's regular classroom.

## STUDENTS IDENTIFIED AS GIFTED

When talking about differentiated instruction, the phrase *what a student needs to be successful* has been repeated several times. It is so critical to clarify here that *successful* does not mean simply mastering a learning outcome or standard. *Successful* means that each student reaches his or her own full potential. Too often, we equate needs with deficits. Gifted students do have needs that are significant and distinct from other students. Yet, because they sometimes do not have an academic deficiency, they tend to be overlooked. Differentiated instruction includes meeting the needs of these students as well. In many cases, the needs of these students require additional challenges, deeper questions, an accelerated pace of learning, or unique learning experiences.

Gifted students provide considerations at each of the 10 steps. When identifying the learning outcomes, it must be questioned if the outcomes will be challenging enough for these learners. When developing a pre-assessment, it must be asked if the tool will allow a student to really reflect all that he or she knows. Instructional considerations must include providing avenues for enrichment as well as increased depth and complexity. These students require the same considerations given to struggling students, and yet these students are often overlooked in the instructional design.

## RELATIONSHIP OF DIFFERENTIATED INSTRUCTION TO RESPONSE TO INTERVENTION

Current trends in education have pushed forward discussions about the response to intervention (RtI) framework and practices. There are many ideas regarding the relationship between this initiative and differentiated instruction. Some sources of information discuss one as being part of the other, and some use the two interchangeably. The reality is that the two are interdependent systems that work hand in hand. RtI focuses on the student's response to instruction and intervention. Differentiated instruction is the instructional response to the student. They are two parts of a circle, creating one whole process of curriculum and instruction. The student response to instruction or intervention is studied and measured. Based on those results, the instruction is differentiated. The student response is again studied and assessed and instruction is adapted to best meet the needs of the student. The process is cyclical (see Figure 10.1).

**Figure 10.1**    The Reciprocal Relationship of Differentiated Instruction and RtI

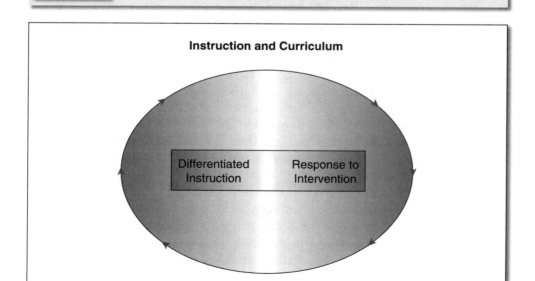

As we move forward with both initiatives in education, we will begin to see this relationship not as two parts but as a turning circle with no beginning and no ending. Both affect the other. Differentiated instruction tells us to use information to plan and deliver instruction. RtI says to study the results of that instruction in order to make more decisions about how to differentiate. Both strongly agree that when a student is not experiencing success, the response must be to identify the causes of the lack of success and provide more supports for the student.

Each of these 10 steps of differentiated instruction can be linked to response to intervention. This chapter started by pointing out that the two commonalities within each of the 10 steps are that (1) all the steps involve systematic, intentional instruction and (2) the responsive nature of these steps blends the intentionality with the gray areas of decision making. RtI helps define those systematic decisions based on data. Again, it is the practice of educators doing research on both the educational strategies and instructional aspects, along with the students themselves, that ensures that students will experience successes in their learning process. As we move forward with both initiatives in education, it is exciting to know that we are moving in a direction that continues to speak of students first. Certainly, nothing matters more.

# *Appendix*

## Differentiated Instruction—The 10-Step Process

Step 1: Examine standards and objectives to be taught. Determine the type of knowledge demanded of the standard and/or objective.

Step 2: Establish the conceptual understanding related to the facts and skills required.

Step 3: For any fact or skill, determine the level of fluency needed for mastery.

Step 4: Design independent student activities that address the facts and skills that are required, along with accommodations for students who need support in achieving mastery of the facts and skills.

Step 5: Reflect on personal knowledge and attitudes related to resources, the content, and the students.

Step 6: Preassess students in the areas of knowledge of facts, skills, conceptual understandings, experiences, attitudes, motivations, and ideas.

Step 7: Determine strategies for instruction at different levels of cognitive processing to include concrete, representational, and abstract processes.

Step 8: Determine the flow of classroom activities to include individual, small-group, and whole-group instruction.

Step 9: Determine benchmarks of student performance and develop tools for ongoing measurement of progress.

Step 10: Develop selections and criteria for the summative product or performance that accurately reflect the intended outcomes of the unit.

## Activities and Conversations for Professional Peer-Learning Communities or Personal Reflection

### Chapter 1

- Think of a time in which you learned something new and went from novice to mastery. This should be an activity or interest of passion for you. Share your learning process, identifying the facts, skills, concepts, principles, and dispositions that you created through your learning. Discuss which levels of learning were the most powerful for you.
- How are these levels of learning similar to or different from other hierarchies with which you are familiar?
- Think of a time you provided opportunities for learning that went beyond the conceptual level for students and allowed them to create their own theories, principles, and generalizations. Share what you did and the learning experiences of the students. Include the students' perspective on the learning experience.

### Chapter 2

- Examine the standards you are currently using in teaching. Identify which are facts, which are skills, and which are concepts. Which are most often addressed?
- Examine state and national standards. What types of knowledge are addressed in these standards? Which are most common?
- Share a time when you learned facts or skills related to a topic without understanding the concepts behind them. What did you have to learn? What limitations did you experience because of the lack of conceptual understanding?
- As a teacher, can you connect the facts and skills you require for mastery to a conceptual understanding? Are there times you accept the students' knowledge of the facts and skills to be enough understanding?

### Chapter 3

- Discuss your use of centers and independent assignments to assist in the development of fluency of facts and skills. Share any technology or other tools to provide independent practice.
- Determine the thought processes you used to determine the level of fluency needed for a fact or skill. Discuss this idea of determining the degree of fluency needed for mastery of a fact or skill. Has this been something that you gave thought to in the past?

- Examine the accommodations you most frequently provide for your students. Are they more often accommodations to the materials, process, or product? Are there new accommodations you are considering?
- Do you consider providing accommodations for students who already have mastery before instruction? What do you do to meet these students' needs when they have already mastered the facts and skills required?
- Using the depth and complexity chart, identify traits you could consider for enrichment opportunities related to a topic or unit of study you are teaching. Create examples that fit your class.

## Chapter 4

- Using the template, complete the self-assessment questions with a professional peer. In what areas can you provide strength for each other? Are there needs you have that are consistent with other professionals as well? Consider possible resources or tools to support your practice.
- Discuss the areas in which you continually survey yourself.
- Discuss the ways in which you survey yourself in the different areas.
- How do you reflect passion in your teaching?
- How do you communicate high expectations of all students? How is this communicated to students who have a history of academically struggling or failing repeatedly?

## Chapter 5

- With a peer, discuss the differences between implementing strategies as preassessment tools and ones that are used for instructional purposes. What indicators can be used to be sure a strategy or tool is implemented for its intended purpose?
- Share some effective preassessment tools you have used that have worked well. Discuss the levels of knowledge assessed.
- Is it essential to have measureable preassessment data? When is it important? When is it not?
- Consider which preassessment tools you find yourself using most often. Do you often assess the same level of knowledge in your preassessments?
- Develop an assessment strategy designed to preassess just facts and skills. Develop a second to preassess conceptual understandings. What are the differences?
- What areas do you most frequently preassess? Background knowledge? Motivation? Habits and work styles?

## Chapter 6

- Using the lesson-planning template provided, complete the elements of a unit plan. Share your plan with a colleague, and request that the peer ask you three questions related to the rationale for specific elements of your plans. Discuss other ideas the peer may have to enhance the plans with research-based strategies or methods that align to the objectives.
- Discuss the elements of the plan that seem natural for you and those which are more challenging.
- Do you have experiences matching strategies and learning processes? Do you often match the outcome to the strategy or just the process?
- If an administrator came into your classroom and asked if you were implementing differentiated instructional practices, how could you show that you are? What does it look like in your classroom? What does it sound like?

## Chapter 7

- Looking at the model of gradual release of responsibility, are there times when you can go directly from modeling to independent practice? What criteria do you use to determine your pace and amount of support to provide at each stage of the gradual release of responsibility?
- Do you differentiate while using the gradual-release model and allow students to move at their own pace? When does that work? When do you want all students at the same pace?
- What instructional strategies do you implement most often to differentiate your whole-group instruction?
- What accommodations do you use most often? How do you know if they are effective?
- How do you most frequently determine the membership in your small-group instruction?
- How often do you provide opportunities for individualized instruction? What management strategies work well for you in helping to make time for working one-on-one with students?

## Chapter 8

- What strategies do you use to monitor student progress? How frequently do you monitor academic progress for any fact or skill? How frequently do you monitor conceptual understandings?
- How do you respond to a learner's physical or mental state each day? What procedures or structures do you have in place in your

classroom that acknowledges your awareness of the students' physical and mental states?

- What elements of the learning environment do you have control of that you have not considered in the past?
- What strategies do you have to allow for accelerated learning of a topic or unit of study in which the student already has advanced knowledge?
- Using the depth and complexity chart from Chapter 3, identify new ways you can provide enrichment to a student who already possesses advanced knowledge.
- Consider the questions you most commonly ask. Which of the four purposes of questioning do they fall into most often? Develop parallel questions for both critical and creative thinking processes. Be sure they both address the same desired learning outcome.
- Discuss how you have used verbs and taxonomies in the past for instructional design. How is the approach different here?

## Chapter 9

- Discuss the types of summative assessments or products you most commonly use. What are the strengths and drawbacks of your choices?
- Examine an assessment developed that requires students to answer closed-ended questions. Are there changes that might be made to make the assessment tool more valid? Using the questions from the closed-ended assessment, change one or two into open-ended prompts. What differences does it make?
- Examine products you have used in the past. Did they align with the learning objective? Did they allow for students to communicate all their learning on the topic?
- Discuss an experience you have had or witnessed in which an assessment was designed to trick, stump, or foster failure rather than provide an opportunity for a person to communicate what he or she knows. What reaction do you have to those assessment experiences?
- Reflect on a rubric you have used or often use. Examine the criteria. Does the top level accurately define highest expectations? Would a parent or student know what the expectations look like from the criteria listed?
- Reflect on the benefits of collaborating with students in creating a rubric.
- Share any resources available that assist with the creation or implementation of rubrics.

# Chapter 10

- Which step of the 10-step process do you find to come most naturally? Which step have you focused on the most in the past? What changes will you make in your own practice?
- Which step is the least comfortable for you? What resources might you seek to increase your comfort in this area?
- Why do you think that students who have been identified as having special needs often are overlooked in the differentiation process? Why is it important to consider the strengths and needs of these students as well?
- Why do you think that students who have been identified as gifted often are overlooked in the differentiation process? Have you considered the needs of students who are gifted when planning your instruction? Why is it important to consider the strengths and needs of these students as well?
- How familiar are you with the response to instruction/intervention (RtI) model? Have you considered the relationship of the RtI model and differentiated instruction? How do you see the two as fitting together?
- What questions about differentiated instruction still remain for you?

**Teacher Self-Assessment: Content**

| Mastery of Content | Self-Rating | | | | |
|---|---|---|---|---|---|
| I can easily explain the concept to another person. | 1 | 2 | 3 | 4 | 5 |
| I am confident in being able to answer questions related to the material. | 1 | 2 | 3 | 4 | 5 |
| I can teach the content through more than one approach. | 1 | 2 | 3 | 4 | 5 |
| *Making Connections* | | | | | |
| I can connect this to a real-world application. | 1 | 2 | 3 | 4 | 5 |
| I can connect this to a concept students have already mastered. | 1 | 2 | 3 | 4 | 5 |
| I can identify elements of the concept that are the same or different than content the students understand. | 1 | 2 | 3 | 4 | 5 |
| *Accuracy of Content* | | | | | |
| I know the most common myths or misconceptions related to the concept. | 1 | 2 | 3 | 4 | 5 |
| I have researched enough about the concept to be able to agree or disagree with secondary sources. | 1 | 2 | 3 | 4 | 5 |
| I know my information is from valid sources. | 1 | 2 | 3 | 4 | 5 |
| I know the vocabulary and terms used by professionals in the field related to the concept. | 1 | 2 | 3 | 4 | 5 |
| *Multiple Perspectives* | | | | | |
| I know the position different groups of professionals take in relation to the concept. | 1 | 2 | 3 | 4 | 5 |
| I know the current issues or topics of the professionals in the field related to the concept. | 1 | 2 | 3 | 4 | 5 |
| I can identify values and/or cultural beliefs in relation to the concept. | 1 | 2 | 3 | 4 | 5 |

## Teacher Self-Assessment: Attitude

| Passion | Self-Rating | | | | |
|---|---|---|---|---|---|
| I am able to verbalize what excites me about the content and share that excitement with students. | 1 | 2 | 3 | 4 | 5 |
| I have multiple ways to share my excitement, including artifacts, visuals, stories, and so on. | 1 | 2 | 3 | 4 | 5 |
| I arrive to class excited to be teaching. | 1 | 2 | 3 | 4 | 5 |
| I am able to verbalize how the content affects me in my own life and can share that impact with students. | 1 | 2 | 3 | 4 | 5 |
| Relevance | | | | | |
| I have personal experiences related to the content. | 1 | 2 | 3 | 4 | 5 |
| I have a story I can share with students to illustrate the content. | 1 | 2 | 3 | 4 | 5 |
| I can identify experiences common to my students that relate to the experiences I have to share. | 1 | 2 | 3 | 4 | 5 |
| Understanding of Students | | | | | |
| I have identified my students' learning styles and know the setting that works best for their learning. | 1 | 2 | 3 | 4 | 5 |
| I know something significant about each student in my class. | 1 | 2 | 3 | 4 | 5 |
| I am able to identify the challenges my students face in their learning as a whole group and as individuals. | 1 | 2 | 3 | 4 | 5 |
| Expectations of Students | | | | | |
| I can articulate the criteria I use to base my expectations of students' performances. | 1 | 2 | 3 | 4 | 5 |
| I can separate achievement of a student and the potential that he or she has. | 1 | 2 | 3 | 4 | 5 |
| I remind myself that any one of my students may be the next one to make a great contribution to the world, and I treat each student in that regard. | 1 | 2 | 3 | 4 | 5 |

## Student Preassessment Areas

**Facts and Skills:**

- Fluency
- Accuracy

**Conceptual Knowledge:**

- Background knowledge
- Current schema
- Perceived relevance

**Affective Factors:**

- Motivation
- Preferred environmental conditions

**Processing:**

- Big picture versus detail
- Doodling versus note taking
- Think time versus talk time

**Resources:**

- Health
- Support systems
- Emotional stability
- Economic well-being
- Cultural understanding

## Framing Template for Strategic Decision Making

| Standard/objective: | |
|---|---|
| **Big idea:** | |
| **Facts or skills:** | **Concepts:** |
| **Level of fluency needed for mastery:**<br><br>☐ Automatic<br>☐ With think time<br>☐ With cues<br><br>**Notes:** | **Background knowledge and other skills required:** |
| **Strategies for practice and support:**<br>(Frequently independent student work) | **Strategies for instruction:** |
| | **Concrete processing:** |
| | Desired outcome:    Strategy: |
| | **Representational processing:** |
| | Desired outcome:    Strategy: |
| | **Abstract processing:** |
| | Desired outcome:    Strategy: |

*(Continued)*

(Continued)

| Management of practice of facts and skills: | Structure for Learning Activities |
|---|---|
| Time period: | Whole group:<br><br>Small group:<br><br>Individual learning: |
| Ongoing assessment tool: | Design for product or performance: |
| Criteria for monitoring progress (targeted skills): | Criteria for exemplary product or performance: |
| Notes: | |

## Tiered Instructional Planning Template

1. Desired learning outcome:

2. Formative assessment:

| **4a.** Supports or accommodations to be provided for struggling learners | **3.** Learning activity or instruction for whole group or on-level learners | **4b.** Adjustments to increase the rigor or intensity of the learning for additional challenge |
|---|---|---|
| | | |

# References

Canfield, J., & Hansen, M. V. (2002). *Chicken soup for the teacher's soul.* Deerfield Beach, FL: Health Communications, Inc.

Heward, W. (1990, Winter). Using response cards to increase student participation in an elementary classroom. *Journal of Applied Behavioral Analysis, 23*(4), 483–490.

Marzano, R. J., Pickering, D. J., & Pollock, J. E. (2004). *Classroom instruction that works: Research-based strategies for increasing student achievement.* Upper Saddle River, NJ: Prentice Hall.

Noguera, P., & Yonemura Wing, J. (2006). *Unfinished business: Closing the racial achievement gap in our schools.* Hoboken, NJ: Jossey-Bass.

Payne, R. (2005). *Framework for understanding poverty.* Highlands, TX: Aha! Process, Inc.

Sahiner, A. (Producer), & Filisky, M. (Writer). (1987). *A private universe* [Motion picture]. Cambridge, MA: Harvard University. (Available from 1-800-LEARNER)

Sullivan, S. S., & Glanz, J. G. (2009). Supervision that improves teaching and learning strategies and techniques (3rd ed.). Thousand Oaks, CA: Corwin.

Tomlinson, C. (2002). *The parallel curriculum: A design to develop high potential and challenge high-ability learners.* Thousand Oaks, CA: Corwin.

Tomlinson, C. (2003). *Differentiation in practice: A resource guide for differentiating curriculum, grades K–5.* Alexandria, VA: Association of Supervision and Curriculum Development.

Tomlinson, C., Kaplan, S. N., Renzulli, J. S., Purcell, J. H., Leppien, J. H., & Burns, D. E. (2001). *Parallel curriculum model.* Thousand Oaks, CA: Corwin.

Wiggins, G., & McTighe, J. (1998). *Understanding by design.* Alexandria, VA: Association of Supervision and Curriculum Development.

Witzel, B. (2003, May). Teaching algebra to students with learning difficulties: An investigation of an explicit instruction model. *Learning Disabilities: Research and Practice, 18*(2), 121–131.

# *Index*